Toshalyn Erve

Black Women Manifesting Greatness Through Education: The Detroit Anthology

Black Women Manifesting Greatness Through Education:
The Detroit Anthology
©2024 Toshalyn Erve

Mo' Betta Digital
41 Avenida Fernando Luis Ribas #449
Utuado, Puerto Rico 00641

ISBN: eBook 978-1-7378873-3-1

ISBN: paperback 978-1-7378873-4-8

First edition: March 2024

REVIEWS

The road to success is never a straight one, as you'll see in the stories of these women. There are many detours along the way, some off the original path and others to a whole new destination never imagined.

Most of the women in this book have had many 'bumps in the road' before arriving where they are today and where they'll be tomorrow.

They all have something in common in that they built a strong foundation through education, hard work and faith, and thus thrived in an environment where many failed.

Although this book is geared to young women of color, everyone can take the lessons learned and apply them to their own lives regardless of age and race.

Hopefully the girls of Detroit and elsewhere will focus on their education and gain the strength and confidence to lead them to achieve whatever they want in life.

- Joan Kirchheimer, retired B&B owner and former architect, Puerto Rico

Black Women Manifesting Greatness: The Detroit Anthology *was an inspiring read! Coming from an equally underserved school system myself, I know the many challenges it can bring. The stories were easy to follow and very informative on how and why they chose their career paths.*

- Tina Favors, Production Associate, Stellantis North America,Oak Park, Michigan

There has never been a better time than now to share a story about women of color who embody the spirit of thriving. In this book, you will explore the stories of 21 women who have successfully journeyed through the Detroit Public School System while navigating through unexpected challenges, cause for pivoting and nonetheless overcoming all obstacles with grace and beauty. What a great source of inspiration for every young woman in the city of Detroit.

- Terrence Southern, CEO of the BlerdOut Movement; Robotics AI Executive; Philanthropist, Dallas, Texas

I know what it's like to grow up in an area where the public schools were a reflection of how the entire system has forgotten about us. I always felt like no matter what I accomplished in life or in my profession, I had come from behind. I certainly didn't have the advantages freely offered to people in wealthier areas. I could absolutely relate to the essays in this wonderful anthology by Toshalyn Erve. They are a huge reminder of what's possible when you combine grit, determination, discipline and parents who push you to succeed. The women behind these powerful stories are proof positive that a system doesn't get to decide a person's trajectory. As Maya Angelou so often said, "And still I rise," and these women are beacons of hope for young women who are current and future attendees of the public school system. No ranking can determine greatness!

- Kristen Chandler, writer and editor, Monroeville, Alabama

I thought the essays were interesting to read! I enjoyed the scripture intros and the anecdotal touches.

- Natalagia Sims, Teacher, Detroit Public Schools Community District, Southfield, Michigan

I think it's inspirational to read about so many successful Black women who are products of Detroit Public Schools Community District. Seeing how each woman used their experiences to guide them after DPSCD was very encouraging. Some of the stories with creative details like the song lyrics for example really drew me in.

- Chad "'Sir Wick Hughes, Ph.D, Director of Bands, Morehouse College, Atlanta, Georgia

Black Women Manifesting Greatness: The Detroit Public School Anthology, *was a refreshing perspective on African American women who attended the public school system in one of America's most dynamic cities, Detroit, Michigan. In the essays, many of the authors spoke of their life experiences—whether it was financial hardships, growing up in rough neighborhoods, or, in some cases, experiencing pregnancies in their teen years. Despite their challenges, these women were ultimately able to overcome the unique obstacles thrown in their paths, and in fact, were able to go on to achieve greatness in their particular fields. Not to mention, they have been a great inspiration to others.*

I found the women's stories to be genuine. Real. They reflected many of the struggles that I myself, as an African American male, have experienced in my own life. They also reminded me of the stories my mother would tell about her experience growing up in the Detroit public schools system.

Overall, I truly enjoyed reading real stories written by real women. Black Women Manifesting Greatness: The Detroit Public School Anthology, *is a book that I would recommend everyone read.*

- Tony Bostick, Stellantis Production Way Specialist, Stellantis, Farmington Hills, Michigan

I dedicate this wonderful book of powerful and inspirational women's stories to my mother, Mrs. Gwendolyn Erve. You are a powerhouse filled with unconditional love, wisdom, kindness and devotion, and even though your story isn't in this book, you are the reason for this entire project because you inspired me to write it. Thank you for always believing in me and continuing to push me to do and be my best. Thank you for always seeing that shining light in me when I couldn't see it in myself and I thank God every day for choosing you to be my mom. I love you!

Love,

Toshalyn

FOREWORD

*"Be not forgetful to entertain strangers: for
thereby some have entertained angels unawares."*
Hebrews 13:2

My mother shared this scripture with me numerous times growing up. The lesson was always to be kind to others because you never know whom you may be speaking to and who they may become. She kept this close to her heart, and it was a guiding truth for her entire career. My mother, Dr. Marjia Lee Mann Cole, was a Detroit Public School principal of Zina Pitcher Elementary for 23 years. For her, every little Black child who walked through that building had the potential to achieve anything they set their mind to. She believed it was her responsibility and her teachers' to instill not only the curriculum but also to inspire these children and their often young parents that they were the descendants of kings and queens, and much was expected. She inspired them to believe that they were the next doctor, nurse, lawyer, or dignitary. Zina Pitcher Elementary was just an ordinary school. It did not have charter or magnet school distinction. But the school was a safe haven for those children and a magical place of potential and promises. Pitcher School was a place where every child had the opportunity to excel.

My education at Detroit Public Schools began at Hampton Elementary in the 1970s. This was the school the New York Times wrote about in 1971 in "Black Students at Former White School in Detroit Learn Racial Pride Along With 3 R's" [sic]. George Romney's kids went there a generation before. The neighborhood that was once known as the "Silk Stocking District," because if you lived there, you must be able to afford silk stockings, was now the focus of white flight and an influx of Black families. However, along with a new community coming into the neighborhood, a new curriculum was also coming. We were not just taught Black history but Black pride each day. It was woven into every aspect of our education and a stark difference to how we were referred to in the private schools I later attended. Pride makes all the difference.

Black teachers are not just educators but also nurturers. Teachers who looked like me and invested in me were a big part of my success. Even after leaving the system, Black female educators from the Detroit Public Schools were my greatest influence because they were my mother's closest friends. They were there for every celebration, every graduation and the hardest days of my life. With great loyalty and love, they attended my graduation from Michigan State College of Human Medicine.

There is a lot to be said about Detroit and Detroit Public Schools. Detroit Public Schools is the lowest-performing urban school system in the United States. It is documented that they have the nation's worst test scores and graduation rates. There are numerous thoughts of why, including absenteeism of teachers and students, stagnant curriculum, financing, internal competition, a struggling city economy, war on drugs and more. The city undoubtedly has been through a lot. However, beneath all this, there are gems and diamonds in the rough that the Detroit Public Schools have produced: Renaissance High School graduate Diawn Jones, chemist, herbalist, and founder of Soza Gym, Martin Luther King High School graduate, Dr. Joslyn Shannon-Harmon, special education supervisor and Cass Tech graduate, Aina Watkins, attorney. These women and the many others you will encounter in this collection are the shining light and pride of an extraordinary, resilient city. I commend Toshalyn Erve, the book's author, for bringing all these incredible women together.

Zina Pitcher Elementary School has since burned down and been demolished. But those teachers still gather to celebrate their bond. Students stay connected on social media and at reunions because they all know they are a part of something special, including my best friend, Stephanie Greenlee Booker. We met in sixth grade and remained close through every milestone of life. My mother gave Stephanie her first job in teaching. These teachers entertained young bright "strangers," from kindergarten through 5th grade, with the most care because they never knew whether they were entertaining Black "angels' ' instead. This foreword is a love letter to my mother, Dr. Marjia Cole, Ed.D. She poured hope, love and pride into many Black students and teachers. She passed away on August 21, 2020, knowing the influence she had on so many families.

As you read the amazing stories in this collection, be mindful of the educators and families that propelled these driven women to where they are today.

Dr. Bridget Cole Williams, MD
Family Physician, Author, Educator
Dr. Bridget MD, LLC
Embody Beauty & Lifestyle
Courage in Cannabis Book Series

Table of Contents

INTRODUCTION

"Education is the most powerful weapon which you can use to change the world. ' Education is one of the most important means of empowering women."

- Nelson Mandela

Education is a powerful tool no matter what race, sex, religion or economic status you are or what part of the world you live in. If you want to be successful at anything, you must educate yourself. According to Dictionary.com, education is the act or process of imparting or acquiring general knowledge, developing the powers of reasoning and judgment, and generally preparing oneself or others intellectually for a mature life. Women have had challenges in educating themselves throughout history in the American educational system. In the early Colonial History of the 17th Century, higher education was designed for men only. Educating women wasn't a priority and was considered unnecessary or dangerous because they were looked at only in domestic roles, which were limited to mostly cooking, cleaning, birthing and raising children. It wasn't until 100 years later, in the 1800s, that women's opportunities and roles in education increased, and they became teachers and learners in formal and informal educational settings.

Before the Civil War in America, a few colleges admitted women[1]. Founded in 1772, Salem College is the oldest known female educational establishment in the U.S.[2], but it did not start awarding college degrees until 1890. Several

---

1   Olson, Janet. "History of Coeducation at Northwestern." Women at Northwestern - Research Guides at Northwestern University. Last updated September 13, 2022. https://lib-guides.northwestern.edu/c.php?g=962006&p=7021136.
2   Salem Academy and College Marks 250th Anniversary - Oldest Educational Institution for Girls and Women in America." Salem College, April 22, 2022. https://old.salem.edu/news/2022/4/salem-academy-and-college-marks-250th-anniversary-oldest-educational-institution-girls.

other all-female student-bodied institutions were founded before the Civil War, including Mount Holyoke College in South Hadley, Massachusetts, founded in 1837 by Mary Lyon as Mount Holyoke Female Seminary; Wesleyan College of Macon, Georgia, founded in 1836 as Georgia Female College and is the first college in the world chartered to grant degrees to women; Queens College (now Queens University) of Charlotte, North Carolina founded in 1857 as Charlotte Female Institute; Averett College (now Averett University) of Danville, Virginia, founded in 1859 as Union Women's College; and Vassar College founded in Poughkeepsie, New York in 1861. With the start of the war and men being away in uniform, opportunities presented themselves for women to fill their roles, and schools and universities became more willing to open their doors to women.

Education was even more difficult for Black women to achieve back then. During this era, Phillis Wheatley was a Black woman credited with being the first African American author of a published book of poetry[3]. Wheatley was born in 1753 in the Gambia, West Africa. She was kidnapped and sold into slavery at the tender age of seven or eight and then transported to North America, where the wealthy and modest Wheatley family of Boston, Massachusetts, bought her. The Wheatleys taught Phillis how to read and write and encouraged her talent in poetry. For a slave owner to educate an enslaved person was unheard of and even verboten, but John Wheatley was known for being a forward thinker and very progressive. By the age of 12, Phillis was reading Greek and Latin classics in their original languages and difficult passages from the Bible.

Because Colonists in America were unwilling to support a Black woman's literature, the Wheatleys sent Phillis to London to get the support she needed to gain success and notoriety. Here, she was not only accepted but adored for both her literary works and her poise. A friend of Susanna Wheatley (Phillis's slave owner's wife), Selina Hastings, the Countess of Huntingdon, funded the publication of Phillis's book Poems on various subjects, Religious and Moral, in late- 1773. Wheatley returned to America to care for Susanna, who was gravely ill. Although Wheatley was set free around the time of her book's publication, and her popularity was at an all-time high, it was still difficult for Phillis as a free woman writer in America. She couldn't secure funding or support for any more of her writing. She became a maid in a local boarding house and died

---

3   Sheridan, Stephanie. "Phillis Wheatley: Her Life, Poetry, and Legacy." National Portrait Gallery. Accessed February 4, 2024. https://npg.si.edu/blog/phillis-wheatley-her-life-poetry-and-legacy.

shortly after, at the age of 31, due to complications from childbirth. In addition to making important contributions to American Literature, Phillis Wheatley's literary and artistic talents helped prove that African Americans were equally intelligent, talented, capable and creative human beings who also benefited from an education.

Throughout our educational history, many Black women have made strides and broke barriers along the way, including Lucy Sessions, who in 1850 became the first African American woman in the U.S. to receive a college degree from Oberlin College[4] (in Ohio).

In 1862, Mary Jane Patterson became the first African American woman to earn a bachelor's degree, also from Oberlin College[5]. In 1864, Rebecca Crumpler became the first African American woman to graduate from a U.S. college with a medical degree and the first and only African American woman to obtain the Doctress of Medicine degree, which she earned from New England Female Medical College of Boston, Massachusetts[6]. In 1879, Mary Eliza Mahoney became the first African American in the U.S. to earn a diploma in nursing, which she earned from The School of Nursing at The New England Hospital for Women and Children in Boston[7].

In 1890, Ida Gray became the first African American woman to earn a Doctor of Dental Surgery degree, which she earned from The University of Michigan[8]. In 1925, beloved poet and author Zora Neale Hurston became the first African American woman to be admitted to Barnard College in New York, New York[9]. In 1931, Jane Matilda Bolin was the first African American woman to graduate

---

4   Gorman, Ron. "William Howard Day & Lucie Stanton." Oberlin Heritage Center Blog, April 2, 2014. https://www.oberlinheritagecenter.org/blog/tag/lucie-sessions/
5   Garner, Carla. "Mary Jane Patterson (1840-1894)." BlackPast, December 3, 2010. https://www.Blackpast.org/african-american-history/patterson-mary-jane-1840-1894/.
6   Rothberg, Emma. "Rebecca Lee Crumpler." National Women's History Museum. October 1, 2021. https://www.womenshistory.org/education-resources/biographies/rebecca-lee-crumpler.
7   Spring, Kelly A. "Mary Eliza Mahoney." National Women's History Museum, 2017. https://www.womenshistory.org/education-resources/biographies/mary-mahoney.
8   Women Who Inspire Us: Ida Gray Nelson Rollins." Center for Women's Health, Oregon Health & Science University. Accessed February 4, 2024. https://www.ohsu.edu/womens-health/women-who-inspire-us-ida-gray-nelson-rollins.
9   Norwood, Arlisha R. "Zora Neale Hurston." National Women's History Museum, 2017. https://www.womenshistory.org/education-resources/biographies/zora-hurston.

from Yale Law School[10]. In 1972, Title IX was passed, making discrimination against any person based on their sex in any federally funded educational program in America illegal[11]. That same year, Willie Hobbs Moore became the first African American woman to earn a Ph.D. in Physics, which she earned from the University of Michigan[12].

These are just a few of the accomplishments Black women have made throughout the years, and it is important that we share their legacies so you know that these tasks are indeed possible to achieve and that we have been achieving them for hundreds of years despite what is written and said about us.

In more recent years, I've noticed a disturbing trend in Black communities across America. We have lost sight of how important education truly is. It's becoming uncool to be smart, attend school and get good grades. Combine this with being a student in the largest failing school district in Michigan, The Detroit Public Schools Community District, and it can create self-confidence issues.

When you're so accustomed to hearing about all the negativity of people and things that impact your district and community and never hear anything positive, you start to question yourself and wonder if successful students can come from institutions with such negative reputations.

Students these days face struggles of day-to-day life and the peer pressure to use drugs, have sex or make alliances with the wrong crowd. It compounds self-confidence issues, particularly when someone is uncertain where their next meal or dollar may come from. And given that Detroit is home to many food deserts, these are well-founded concerns.

My friends, I am here to tell you there is hope. Through all your trials, tribulations and struggles, there is still the opportunity for you to be successful, just as I was. When I was about your age, I struggled with many of these same issues, but through a lot of hard work and prayer, I achieved one of my dreams of becoming a published author, and there are many more stories in this book just like mine. All of these wonderful women are graduates of The Detroit Public

10   Monroe, Lisa A. "Jane Bolin." The Yale & Slavery Research Project. Accessed February 4, 2024. https://yaleandslavery.yale.edu/jane-bolin.
11   14th Amendment and the Evolution of Title IX." United States Courts. Accessed February 4, 2024. https://www.uscourts.gov/educational-resources/educational-activities/14th-amendment-and-evolution-title-ix.
12   Shirley Ann Jackson: From Theoretical Physicist to MIT's First African-American Woman to Earn a Doctorate." American Institute of Physics. https://www.aip.org/sites/default/files/history/files/AIP-Hobbs-Jackson-Handout.pdf.

Schools Community District and were able to achieve their dreams, but the road wasn't easy. However, anything worth achieving is never easy, right?

I have added questions at the end of each essay designed to help you in your reflection. There are obviously no right or wrong answers. My intention is to get you thinking critically about their essays and how you can apply the answers to your own journey.

I hope that by reading this book, you will gain some much-needed confidence in yourself and inspiration through our stories that will motivate you to continue to follow your dreams no matter how impossible they seem to be right now.

Brittany Rhodes

"For I know the plans I have for you,"
declares the Lord, "plans to prosper you
and not to harm you, plans to give you
hope and a future." Jeremiah 29:11

I begged my mother not to send me to Renaissance High School in Detroit, Michigan. I wanted to go to Cass Technical High School (Cass), where some of my friends went. My mom was not having it. She was a K-8th grade Principal at a Detroit charter school at the time, so, needless to say, she knew a lot about the educational landscape in the city. And her mind was already made up. She liked that Renaissance was small and felt it would be a better fit for me (but let me be clear: she still loves Cass as that's her alma mater). Before I started high school, we would ride past Renaissance, and she would playfully taunt me saying, "Say hello to your new school!" When I first started at Renaissance, she looked at me and said, "Let me know when you start liking it."

Six weeks later, I sheepishly told her that I liked it.

At Renaissance, I was involved in several activities. I was on the newspaper staff for one year and the yearbook staff for two years. I also played volleyball for one year. I wish I had started playing before high school; I liked playing volleyball but was not good at it and didn't make it past junior varsity!

But one thing I was good at was math. Yes, you read that right–mathematics! In my ninth-grade year, my Algebra teacher noticed my aptitude for math and recommended me for a special track that would allow me to take Geometry AND Algebra II in tenth grade. Typically, students did not take Algebra II until eleventh grade, but I was placed in both math classes the following year because of my grades and excitement for math. In eleventh grade, I took Pre-Calculus; in twelfth grade, I took AP (Advanced Placement) Calculus AB, a class designed to be the equivalent of a first-semester college calculus course.

Around this time, my mom suggested that I major in Math in college. I looked at her in disbelief and asked, "Who would do such a thing?! Who would go to college and major in MATH?" It was one of the most absurd things my teenage ears had ever heard. Little did I know I would be eating those words in a few years.

But before I talk about that, let me go back a little bit.

When I was in the tenth grade, the Detroit NAACP (National Association for the Advancement of Colored People) hosted a Black College Tour during Spring Break. I, along with many friends and associates from schools all over the city, eagerly signed up. I was vaguely familiar with HBCUs (Historically Black Colleges and Universities) but had never visited one. I was so excited to visit these wonderful institutions, which were originally created to provide higher education opportunities to Black people when we were not allowed to attend white schools. So, off we went. Several charter buses full of rowdy Detroit kids and our chaperones descended to the South to visit Florida A&M University (FAMU), Tennessee State University, the Atlanta University Center (which included Spelman College, Morehouse College, Clark Atlanta University and Morris Brown College at the time), and several other dynamic HBCUs. Initially, I had my heart set on FAMU. But when we got to Atlanta, I felt an immediate connection to the city. I don't know what it was, but I felt like I belonged there. When we visited Spelman, I knew I was home!

Two years later, I began my first year at Spelman College. My major was a dual degree in Computer Science and Engineering. I planned to spend the first three years at Spelman, majoring in Computer Science, and two more at Georgia Tech, majoring in Computer Engineering. I would have two Bachelor's degrees in five years! I was ready! But after the first few months, I realized coding/engineering was not something I wanted to pursue as a career. That's one of the beautiful things about college (and life in general)—you can pivot anytime! I thought about what I should change my major to, and Math immediately rose to the top of my mind.

You probably already know where I'm about to go with this.

I called my mom and sheepishly told her that I was changing my major to Math (remember when I was in eleventh grade and she suggested I major in math, and I acted like it was the worst idea ever? Yeah, there I was again, eating my words! Mom, why were you always right?!).

Anyway, in my sophomore year of college, I began tutoring other college students in math. I fell in love with tutoring. As you probably know, many people don't like math (you may even be one of those people, though I hope not)! They find it hard, confusing and irrelevant. I fell in love with tutoring because it allowed me to show people that math can be fun and make sense!

Despite my best efforts, I graduated from college in 2006 without a job lined up. Thankfully, I had a skill that I could immediately monetize–and that was math tutoring! From then on, tutoring was my side hustle. Besides a two-year tutoring break while I earned my Master of Business Administration (MBA) from the Tepper School of Business at Carnegie Mellon University in Pittsburgh, Pennsylvania, I was always tutoring. Even after I graduated from business school, spent some time living and working in Nashville and Washington D.C., and moved back home to Detroit to work in the nonprofit world and do my part to better the city, you could find me tutoring on the side. Because there's a high demand for math tutors, we can charge a high hourly rate (like $75/hour and up!), but I have always charged way lower than that because I want to help as many children who look like me as I can. I don't want money (or lack thereof) to be the reason why a child doesn't get a shot at the math confidence we all deserve.

At some point, after I moved back to Detroit, I took a short break from tutoring because work was so busy. One day, I mentioned to my boyfriend (now my husband) that I missed tutoring. Almost immediately, he found a job posting online from a youth organization on the East side called the Downtown Boxing Gym (DBG)–and they were looking for a part-time math tutor! I applied, interviewed and got the job! At DBG, our students come from all over the Detroit area and go to various schools–some DPSCD, some charter, some suburbs, etc. After working there for a short time, I noticed that too many of my students, no matter where they went to school, had low math confidence and high math anxiety. The struggle wasn't with higher-level math like Algebra or Trigonometry, though. Many struggled with basic math–fractions, decimals, negative numbers, etc. They were familiar with these concepts but hadn't mastered them, which made math feel much harder than it should have.

At that point, I started thinking about how I could address this problem on a wider scale. I was having great success with my students, but I was also acutely aware that it wasn't just Detroit students who struggled with math; in fact, 93% of American adults have math anxiety (that they got when they were kids)! I knew I had to do my part to help fix this. Math is quite useful; we use it to cook, bake, shop, budget–basically to live! On top of that, being both skilled at and confident in math can be very lucrative and rewarding. So, for people, especially girls and Black people, to be considered by some as inferior in math and not to feel confident in it is a huge problem for me. With my gift for helping people understand and enjoy math, I knew I had to do something.

That's how my business, Black Girl MATHgic, was born! Black Girl MATHgic is a movement to increase math confidence, persistence and assistance in children, focusing on girls and Black children disproportionately impacted by high math anxiety. My business' main product is a monthly subscription box called the Black Girl MATHgic box. (Have you ever seen those commercials where they send boxes with food and recipes to your house every month, and the people in the commercial cook the food and have a good old meal? That's a subscription box. Instead of food, I put math activities, stories about women mathematicians, and other cool math stuff in my box).

Since I launched Black Girl MATHgic in 2019, we have shipped over 1,200 boxes to over 35 states and Canada, won almost $20,000 from grants and pitch competitions, shown hundreds of kids that they have what it takes to be math stars and been featured in major outlets like Beyonce's website!

I could not have done this at the level I have been able to without my Detroit upbringing and DPSCD education. Detroit laid the foundation for me to pursue greatness. I was more than prepared for college thanks to my DPSCD education, and college was the springboard to my business origin story because it's where I began tutoring math.

Plus, I am literally using every experience I've ever had to run my business. I use my journalism experience from the high school newspaper and yearbook to interview the mathematicians I feature in the box each month. I use my experience working as Director of Community Engagement at Belle Isle (my last job before I started Black Girl MATHgic) to leave a positive impression every time I interact with my customers and supporters. I use my graduate degree in business to understand marketing, social media, finance, operations and more.

And you already know I use my math skills!

I use my math skills on everything from measuring the items I want to put in the box to making sure they will fit in the box to weighing the boxes to making sure they stay under a pound (shipping goes up $3 if it goes over!) to calculating my profit margin each month.

And I would be using math in my business even if my business weren't focused on helping kids feel good about their math ability–because math is EVERYWHERE in business!

Even though at times I got caught up in the comparison game (quick note: don't do it!) and couldn't understand why I wasn't getting the opportunities or money other people were getting when I was putting in the work, once I started Black Girl MATHgic, it all made sense. Everything I went through, good or bad, has prepared me for this moment. Everything came full circle. So, even if something seems pointless or annoying in your life, know that you're going through it for a reason. Your hard work WILL pay off.

Brittany Rhodes
Founder Black Girl MATHgic

Brittany Rhodes is a math tutor/coach, former GED Math Instructor, and Founder and General MATHager of Black Girl MATHgic (BGM). BGM is a movement dedicated to increasing math confidence, awareness, enthusiasm, identity, fluency and persistence in children, with a focus on girls and black children. BGM's flagship products are the Black Girl MATHgic Monthly Box and The MATHgic Prince Quarterly Box, the first and only subscription boxes designed to increase math confidence and decrease math anxiety in children on a 3rd-8th grade math level. Brittany received her Bachelor of Science in Mathematics from Spelman College and her Master of Business Administration in Marketing, Communication, and Organizational Behavior from the Tepper School of Business at Carnegie Mellon University. Brittany is a proud native of Detroit, where she lives with her husband and daughter.

QUESTIONS

1. **Embracing Change:** Brittany initially resisted attending Renaissance High School but later found value in the experience. Reflect on a time when you were hesitant about a change or decision. How did it turn out, and what did you learn from it?

2. **Finding Your Strengths:** Brittany discovered her aptitude for math, which significantly influenced her career path. Think about your own strengths and interests. How can you utilize them to shape your future?

3. **The Role of Mentorship:** Brittany's mother played a pivotal role in guiding her educational choices. Discuss the influence of mentors in your life. How have they helped shape your decisions and perspectives?

4. **Navigating Career Shifts:** Brittany's journey from college to founding Black Girl MATHgic involved several career shifts. What does her story teach you about adaptability and openness to new opportunities?

5. **Impact of Educational Tours:** Brittany's visit to HBCUs was a turning point in her education. How can exploring educational institutions beyond your immediate environment broaden your perspectives and opportunities?

6. **Starting a Business:** Brittany used her skills and experiences to start a business addressing math anxiety. If you were to start a business or initiative, what problem would you want to address, and how would you use your skills to do so?

7. **Overcoming Challenges:** Despite facing joblessness after college, Brittany found a way to monetize her skills. Share a challenge you've faced and how you addressed or could address it creatively.

8. **Community Engagement:** Brittany's work focuses on uplifting others through education. In what ways can you contribute to your community or a cause you care about?

9. **Learning from Every Experience:** Brittany applies lessons from every part of her life to her business. How can you use your past and present experiences to benefit your future goals?

10. **Hard Work and Resilience:** Brittany's story exemplifies hard work and resilience. Discuss a goal you're working towards. How do her experiences inspire you to approach your challenges and ambitions?

Sommer Oliver

"For God hath not given us the spirit of fear; but of power, and of love, and of a sound mind." II Timothy 1:7

My name is Sommer Oliver, and I'm an Atlanta-based production coordinator with 15-plus years of experience in the television/film industry. I'm a native Detroiter: What up, doe! Many, many, many moons ago, I graduated from the illustrious Cass Technical High School.

Cass Tech was a college preparatory high school; during my first year, I had to select a "curriculum" similar to selecting a major for college. My curriculum was Performing Arts. The Performing Arts Curriculum at Cass was outstanding. Growing up, I wanted to be in front of someone's camera as an actress or a talk show host. So, there was no other option for high school: Cass Tech was it. Period!

There, I learned about theater, various acting techniques, stage direction and the basics of film production. I was a producer, writer and cast member of the renowned PA Guild (Performing Arts Guild). The PA Guild was our version of In Living Color, Saturday Night Live, or Wild 'n Out. Students had to audition to become a member. Several rounds of auditions were open to the entire student body, but only a few open spots were available in the PA Guild. It was intense but more than worth it for those who made it. The PA Guild put on shows once or twice a semester. Students were charged admission to attend, and we would sell out every single time. If TikTok, YouTube, or any other social media platform had existed, we would've gone viral.

After graduating from Cass Tech, I attended Clark Atlanta University in Atlanta, Georgia, where I majored in the Atlanta club life. I went out literally every night and barely made it to my classes. My club outings decreased during my junior and senior years once I began taking film/media electives.

During my senior year, my entire film class interned on an independent film titled "Trois 2". It was a huge deal because the up-and-coming producer and rising director were both young Black men and barely out of college themselves. Their names were Rob Hardy and Will Packer. This was the first time I had ever been on a film set and learned about the various departments, paperwork, etc. that went into making a film.

Fun Fact: years later, I worked again with both the rising director Rob Hardy on Season 2 of a BET (Black Entertainment Television) show called Being Mary Jane and with up-and-coming producer Will Packer briefly on The OWN (Oprah Winfrey Network) network drama Ambitions. Full circle moments for me, for sure.

By the grace of God, I managed to graduate from Clark Atlanta University on time with a Bachelor of Arts degree in Mass Media Arts with a concentration in film. Upon graduating, unlike my peers, I did not have multiple job offers pending and grad school was a hard no.

So, I remained in Atlanta and got a "regular" job at Costco Wholesale. While working at Costco, I was able to book some Production Assistant (PA) gigs on a few music videos. This was when record labels/production companies had million-dollar-plus budgets.

Those PA gigs were the beginning of my TV/film journey. I quickly learned that securing jobs in this industry was all about who you knew first and experience second. In addition to the music videos, I booked days and weeks here and there on a few feature films. Very few people of color were working behind the scenes, if any at all.

Eventually, I took a leave of absence from Costco to work as an office production assistant on Tyler Perry's film Why Did I Get Married. Before working at Tyler Perry Studios, I had not worked on a studio film with Black department heads, producers or directors.

As an office PA (an entry-level position), my duties included answering phones, handling calls for my production coordinator and producers, office runs (picking up snacks for the office, fetching Starbucks), and shipping and logging incoming/outgoing packages.

Once production wrapped on Why Did I Get Married, I was offered another job at Tyler Perry Studios. Then I decided to step out on faith, quit my regular job at Costco and work full-time as a freelancer in the film industry. A freelancer in the film industry doesn't work for just one set production company or service. Instead, they hire out their expertise to companies or individuals.

On my next gig, I worked as a casting assistant. Casting assistants provide general administrative duties in the production office and assistance during casting sessions when actors perform screen tests on camera. I didn't know then, but my work experience as a production assistant proved useful in this role. From there, I transitioned back to the production office and eventually became a production coordinator.

Production coordinators are the gatekeepers of studio policies/procedures. Our office distributes all the production paperwork (call sheets, scripts, schedules, etc.). We make travel arrangements for all distant crew members and cast in town and set up their accommodations. I am responsible for preparing, updating and distributing crew lists (a list of the filmmaking team members responsible for making the film) and daily progress reports and script changes. We provide mobile offices, stages, and other equipment necessary for successful film production. We also make sure that all cast members and equipment are insured. Exciting stuff, right? Seriously, that is just a small portion of what my team and I handle daily. The production office is the communication hub for all shows. It interfaces with literally every department. I learned and am still learning "the business" of television and film in this office.

There is often this perception that the TV/film industry is all glitz and glam; you meet all these exciting people, and it's so much fun. People have no idea about all the hard work, countless hours, and number of people it takes to create a one-hour film or television show. It is a BIG business and not for the faint of heart. I have missed a lot of graduations, birthday parties, and performances due to my grueling work schedule.

However, I am honored to have been an integral part of some amazing projects, especially the ones produced by people who look like me. I've had the pleasure of working with and meeting Tyler Perry, Oprah Winfrey, Ava Duvernay and Mara Brock Akil, just to name a few. All visionaries and heavy hitters in the television and film industry.

I've most recently worked as the production coordinator on the Starz Network episodic P-Valley, Good Universe's feature film Blockers and season one of the Warner Horizon episodic Queen Sugar. I love to challenge myself and learn something new from every production experience. After being in this industry for over a decade, I feel like I'm just getting started as I'm transitioning into yet another role. Stay tuned…

Everyone's story is different, and one of the beautiful things about this business, unlike other careers, is there's no preset instruction or route. After identifying your desired path, you determine what's next, not the industry! You can literally be a production assistant today, and a producer tomorrow-you never know. The sky's the limit.

So, with that being said, if you want to be a producer, start now! You can start researching producers on films you like, take an accounting course and learn about budgets. Or if you want to be a costume designer, director, set decorator or producer, look into what it takes to become successful in that position. Find out who the costume designers, directors, etc., are on your favorite projects. Check out the Internet Movie DataBase (IMDB), which is an online database of information related to films, television series, podcasts, home videos, video games, and streaming content online–including cast, production crew and personal biographies, plot summaries, trivia, ratings, and fan and critical reviews. IMDb began as a fan-operated movie database on the Usenet group "rec.arts. movies" in 1990 and moved to the Web in 1993. Since 1998, it has been owned and operated by IMDb.com, Inc., a subsidiary of Amazon. IMDB and Google are your friends.

No matter the path you choose, you'll need to do your research, be resourceful and be willing to put in that work! It's important to be a team player with a positive attitude to have positive work experiences. These experiences allow you to expand your network, receive continuous job offers, and create lasting relationships.

Sommer Oliver

FreeLance Production Coordinator

Sommer Oliver is an Atlanta-based production coordinator with over 15 years in the TV/film industry. A Detroit native and Cass Technical High School alumna, she pursued Performing Arts before attending Clark Atlanta University. Sommer's career began with internships and PA roles, evolving through experiences on sets like Tyler Perry's Why Did I Get Married to her current role, where she's worked on projects like P-Valley and Queen Sugar. Known for her adaptability and dedication, Sommer's journey reflects the importance of networking, versatility, and the relentless pursuit of one's passion in the competitive entertainment industry.

QUESTIONS

1. **Reflecting on Paths Taken:** How does Sommer's journey from performing arts in high school to production coordination challenge or inspire your views on career development and passion?

2. **The Role of Education and Experience:** In what ways does Sommer's college experience illustrate the balance between formal education and real-world experience in shaping a career?

3. **Networking and Opportunity:** Sommer emphasizes the importance of networking in the film industry. Reflect on your own career or aspirations. How do you view the role of networking in achieving professional goals?

4. **Career Transitions:** Sommer transitioned from a "regular" job to a full-time freelancer in the film industry. What insights can you draw from her experience about taking risks and making significant career changes?

5. **Industry Perceptions vs. Reality:** Sommer discusses the misconception of the TV/film industry as all "glitz and glam." How does this contrast with your perceptions of this or other industries?

6. **The Impact of Representation:** How important do you think representation behind the scenes (e.g., Black department heads, producers, directors) is in the film and TV industry, based on Sommer's experiences?

7. **Learning and Growing in a Career:** Sommer mentions always learning something new from every production experience. How does lifelong learning influence career growth and satisfaction in your opinion?

8. **Aspirations and Achieving Dreams:** Considering Sommer's advice to start now if you want to be a producer (or any other role), how does this speak to your own aspirations and the steps you're taking to achieve them?

9. **The Value of Teamwork and Attitude:** Reflect on Sommer's emphasis on being a team player with a positive attitude. How do these qualities contribute to success in any career?

10. **Exploring Unique Career Paths:** Sommer's story highlights a non-linear career path. How does her journey inspire you to think about your own career path, especially if you're considering a less traditional route?

Caron Recker

"She is clothed with strength and dignity, and she laughs without fear of the future." Proverbs 31:25

High School was not easy for me; I thank God he gave me the strength to graduate. I entered Martin Luther King Jr. Senior High School in the fall of 1992 in the Math Science and Applied Technology Program (MSAT). My first year was a struggle because I didn't have discipline or a study regimen, and it showed. I was removed from the MSAT Program because of my academic performance. I was allowed back into the MSAT program my sophomore year but was on probation due to my grades. In my junior year, I left Martin Luther King High School to attend a high school for pregnant girls and teen moms. Yes, I was pregnant at the age of 17. I had my daughter that summer and returned to Martin Luther King High School under the normal high school curriculum, losing my place in the MSAT Program. I graduated from high school by the skin of my teeth, with my one-year-old daughter at my graduation ceremony.

Now that I had completed high school with a child, I had to grow up. I applied to Wayne State University and started the application process to become a police officer with the Detroit Police Department. However, mentally, I still wasn't ready for school. My mother was not happy with my decision to become a police officer for the City of Detroit, so she did everything in her power to get me to quit the academy, and eventually, I did. It had been over two years since I graduated from high school, and I was still trying to find my way. I wasn't successful at Wayne State University because I was a young mother. I worked as a cashier and waitress, but I knew I needed to do more to establish a great future for my daughter. I ended up pregnant again with my second daughter, and six months later, I started the next chapter of my life working at Ameritech.

I started my first real job at Ameritech in September 1998, but less than six months later, I went back to school because I knew I needed to gain the skills and credentials needed for a successful career. When I first consulted with the counselor at Wayne County Community College, he recommended that I take pharmaceutical classes. My first reaction was "no, thank you," I'm not interested in that, but I was interested in being a teacher. He really tried to convince me, but I didn't listen. I took general courses for the first year that I knew would transfer to Wayne State University because I planned to get back into Wayne State University. My educational interest changed from teaching to electrical engineering technology. Once I realized I found my groove and this engineering stuff was for me, I continued taking engineering classes at Wayne County Community College. I took classes at any campus that offered the courses I needed for my electrical engineering technology major.

During my Wayne County Community College days, I learned some valuable lessons. One lesson I'll never forget came from Mr. Raymond Card. I met Mr. Card while applying for a scholarship with Emerson Process Management. This company led in the supply of process management products and automation systems. Applicants had to go through a phone and in-person interview. I nailed the phone interview. My peers were going to be allowed to go into the in-person interview with me because I spoke on their behalf during the phone interview to ensure that they got interviews as well. I was so nervous to finally get a face-to-face interview. I had a new suit, and I was ready! When I arrived for the interview, I saw some of my peers. We were all in the waiting room together when my name was called. I was led into Mr. Card's office by his assistant.

I was immediately embarrassed because he would not interview me. I wanted to cry, but I had to hold back my tears. He excused the other interviewees in the office with us and closed the door. He made me take a seat and explained that I needed to change my hairstyle because, as a Black woman, I was already going to have challenges. As a Black woman with red braids, I would never be taken seriously until I presented myself in a professional manner. He talked to me for about 20 minutes and then excused me from his office. His assistant scheduled another interview date for me, and I left. I sat in my car for about five minutes and cried from the embarrassment I caused myself by missing out on an opportunity like this because of my appearance. It was then that I realized I didn't blow the interview because of my appearance but my actions and choices because I chose to go and get this hairstyle just before the interview. I also realized that the interview wasn't blown; I had a second chance because the interview had already been rescheduled. I drove home and took those red braids out!

The Emerson interview was life-changing. Deciding to remove the braids opened the door for me to be a scholarship recipient and helped shape me into the professional woman I am today. Mr. Card became not only my sponsor but also my mentor and friend. He told me that every successful student should always have a sponsor and a mentor. Mr. Card was that for me; he even attended my undergraduate graduation from Wayne State University. I remember a conversation I had with Mr. Card about obstacles and fears. He explained that whenever you have obstacles or fears, you must put yourself in situations that give you opportunities to get through them. He overcame his obstacles with this philosophy, and I eventually overcame mine. My fear was public speaking. Because of his advice, I spoke at my graduation, and I always found myself volunteering for opportunities to speak in front of groups. Now, you would not know that I feared public speaking because I always speak in front of large groups.

After graduation, I started my career at Fiat Chrysler Automobiles (FCA), now Stellantis in March 2006. I was hired at Global Engine Manufacturing Alliance (GEMA), now the Dundee Engine Plant (DEP). The GEMA plant was a joint venture with Chrysler, Mitsubishi, and Hyundai. Hyundai pulled out, and the plant eventually became another Chrysler plant. The ideal state of this plant was very different, starting with the hiring process. The applicants had to have a degree or at least eight years of manufacturing experience. I didn't have any experience, but I had a degree. There was also a test and a panel interview with three to four leadership members from the facility. This was an intense process, but I got the position! I was hired as an operator on the machining line. The block line is where I started my FCA career. I was an operator for just under a year; then, I was promoted to electrical engineer for the headline. As the headline electrical engineer, I provided technical support for the line, working with the production and maintenance teams and any projects assigned to me. I left the company a year later and went into the steel industry.

The steel industry was much different than the automotive industry. I worked in two different steel mills, which were as different as night and day. The first steel mill was Mac Steel, a bar steel mill plant in Jackson, Michigan. The environment was very hot and dirty. I was an electrical project engineer and had the opportunity to work on several projects before the plant was closed. I then accepted my next position at ATI Allegheny in Louisville, Ohio, as a cold roll finish process control engineer. I managed the rolling mills, slitters and packaging line and worked with maintenance on any electrical breakdowns or projects. I was then promoted to plant automation support engineer, and in this position, I supported the entire plant. My final role at ATI Allegheny Ludlum was Senior operations leader of the Anneal and Pickling Department. I was promoted three times at Alleghany in three years before returning to Michigan to be closer to my family.

In July 2012, I moved back to Michigan and took on a role as an electrical controls engineer back at FCA's Dundee Engine Plant, where my engineering career began. I was hesitant about returning home because things were going so well at ATI. However, my daughters didn't think it was fair that I took them away from our family, so it was time to go back home. It was a very humbling experience for me to return home to the same role I had left. Still, I decided to take any position just to return to Michigan, and I knew I could move up from there.

After being home for almost three months, I was working late one evening because of a major breakdown. Once everything was put back together, I took advantage of that time to have a one-on-one conversation with the manufacturing manager. I opened the door to the conference room where he was working and asked if I could have five minutes of his time; he gave me 10. I explained to him that I aspired to have his job. I mentioned that I knew I had only been back for three months and that promotions take time, but I asked for his perspective on how long it should take for me to get promoted. He reminded me that I had only been back with the company for three months, and normally, they wouldn't even consider me releasable until I had been in my role for at least 18 months. I told him I understood and I just wanted him to be aware of my goals and interests. I left feeling satisfied that I took full advantage of the opportunity to talk to him. A couple of weeks later, I was presented with a job offer as an area manager over the north machining lines, which I accepted. I stayed in that role for three years, then transitioned from powertrain to the assembly group.

In August 2015, I started the next chapter of my career in the Assembly Division at the Jefferson North Assembly Plant (JNAP) as the Chassis Area Manager.

Coming from powertrain, this was a much different pace and environment for me. Initially, I was intimidated because of the size of the plant and not knowing the assembly build process. I had to utilize my strengths to be just as successful in assembly as I was in powertrain. I started reviewing the budget to understand what my scrap issues were. I walked the process and production lines with the workstations printed out to learn the people and familiarize myself with the vehicle-building process. I was in this position for 15 months. I was then offered a position as the plant's world-class manufacturing lead, working directly with the plant manager. I accepted the position and the challenge of acquiring the World Class Manufacturing (WCM) Bronze Award.

World Class Manufacturing (WCM), is a methodology used by FIAT CHRYSLER (FCA). This methodology is based on continuous improvement in the performance of the corporate Operating System to achieve World Class competitiveness. In World Class Manufacturing, there are three levels a plant can achieve based on points received in a yearly audit. They are bronze, silver, and gold—each level signifies improvements in several key metrics such as cost reduction, productivity, efficiency, significant reduction in workplace injuries and quality improvements to name a few. It is very difficult to reach bronze status and there were only a few plants in North America that had achieved this.

The JNAP journey to accomplish the WCM Bronze Award started in 2010, and in November 2018, we finally achieved it.

I continued to work as the WCM Lead until June 2019. I was asked to lead a special project with FCA, the City of Detroit and Southeastern High School. During this project, I oversaw community events and internship programs. I built a network bridge with Southeastern High School and FCA at both Jefferson and the Mack Engine plants. In March 2020, I took on a new role as the World Class Manufacturing Central Team Professional Maintenance Lead for North America. This is my current role, and it is very exciting. I joined the team at a time when I could be very instrumental in changes currently being developed and implemented throughout the company. This is the first role I've held that allows me to support multiple plants and not be confined to just one location. I support plants in the United States, Canada and Mexico. This is not the position I envisioned after the WCM Lead, but I am so glad I was offered and accepted the position. I now have a normal sleep pattern and have slowed down to enjoy life with my family.

I want to leave you with a lesson I learned. Until recently, I always set my goals based on positions or titles. After having a few disappointments and being misled, I learned that what God has for me is for me, and no one can take that away. This has led me to refocus my professional aspirations away from chasing titles to focus on always being effective in whatever position I'm in. I aim to learn everything I can to pass that knowledge on to my team. I also want to leave my footprint in every position as I move to the next opportunity. I think that the world has so many opportunities available to us all. It's all about how we apply ourselves, take the ride and enjoy learning along the way. And remember, in anything you do, always leave your footprint by leaving the job or team better than you found them.

Caron Recker

Senior Manager of General Assembly Stellantis

A lifelong Detroiter, Caron Recker has spent much of her manufacturing career working at the two plants in the heart of the city, making an impact not only on the shop floor but in the community. Recker has held many roles at both Detroit Assembly Complex – Jefferson and its sister plant, Mack Assembly in 2022, she was promoted to her current role as North America Stellantis Production Way shop director for general assembly, responsible for implementing the Company's new manufacturing system across the assembly plants.

Recker is passionate about developing the next generation of manufacturing leaders. She helped establish an Advanced Manufacturing Academy at Detroit's Southeastern High School and every summer hosts Southeastern students as part of an internship program at the Detroit Assembly Complex. The program she developed educates students about careers in manufacturing while building life skills like conflict resolution and money management.

"I love seeing a light turn on in the students' minds," Recker said. "When they get engaged, I know that's the future of our industry."

Recker encourages students to always keep a goal in mind, have a plan and stay on track. "It's never too late to start," she said. "You might not start young, you might be derailed, but you can always restart. Don't ever stop trying."

In addition to supporting students, Recker is also co-chair of Stellantis' Women in Manufacturing Business Resource Group. Recker believes Stellantis is advancing roles for women in manufacturing, with an increased focus on diversity. "There are new initiatives implemented for marginalized groups such as Black women," she said.

QUESTIONS

1. **Overcoming Early Challenges:** Caron faced significant challenges during her high school years. Reflect on a difficult period in your life. How did you overcome these challenges, and what strengths did you discover about yourself?

2. **The Impact of Life Changes:** Becoming a parent at a young age significantly altered Caron's path. How have major life changes influenced your decisions and goals?

3. **Pursuing Education Amidst Adversity:** Despite obstacles, Caron continued her education and shifted her career focus. Discuss the importance of perseverance in education and career, especially when facing personal challenges.

4. **Valuing Mentorship and Guidance:** Caron's experience with Mr. Card was transformative. How can mentors and advisors impact your personal and professional development? Have you had a similar experience?

5. **Career Progression and Adaptability:** Caron's career journey showcases adaptability and growth. How does her story inspire you to approach your career development, especially when facing setbacks or new opportunities?

6. **Professional Presentation and Perception:** Caron learned a valuable lesson about professional appearance and perception. In what ways do you think presentation and personal branding are important in your chosen field or career aspirations?

7. **Setting and Refocusing Goals:** Caron shifted her focus from pursuing titles to being effective in her roles. How can you apply this mindset to your own goals and aspirations?

8. **The Importance of Effective Communication:** Public speaking was initially a fear for Caron, but she overcame it. Discuss the role of communication skills in personal and professional success. How can you improve or leverage your communication skills?

9. **Work-Life Balance:** Caron speaks about finding a balance and enjoying life with her family. How do you plan to balance your professional ambitions with personal life and self-care?

10. **Leaving a Positive Impact:** Caron emphasizes leaving a positive footprint in every role. What does leaving a positive impact mean to you, and how do you plan to achieve it in your endeavors?

Christie Hogue

God says, "For I know the plans I have for you, declares the Lord, plans to prosper you and not to harm you, plans to give you hope and a future." Jeremiah 29:11

Many people view life differently. As Rick Warren described in the book Purpose Driven Life, some people view life as a carousel, some as a deck of cards, and some, like me, view it as a journey. There is a quote by an anonymous author that states: *A strong woman has faith that she is strong enough for the journey...but a woman of strength has faith that it is in the journey that she will become strong."*

There are three most influential people in my life: my grandmother, my father and my mother. I am the granddaughter of a woman who was blessed to reach the age of 100 years old. My grandmother's perseverance and creative ways were unbelievable; she maintained a healthy lifestyle by staying abreast of what was happening. She kept us on our toes until she passed away just two weeks shy of her 101st birthday. I am grounded as the daughter of a Vietnam Veteran who gives me those "straight talk, no chaser" talks. My dad also gave me the sensitivity I needed when working with my veteran patients, helping me understand that everyone has a story. I am also grounded as the daughter of a God-fearing woman. My mom instilled in me that with God, all things are possible. She has taught me the importance of determination, given the three careers she has achieved. She graduated high school in South Carolina early and pursued a college degree despite her father's belief that girls weren't supposed to attend college. Her mother saw and supported her will to pursue her education by selling cows to put her through school. My mom became a teacher and taught high school French and Spanish for 30 years, retiring at 55 from the Detroit

Public School System. She then went on to teach at our local community college (Wayne County Community College) and returned to school to pursue her Doctorate in Ministry at age 65.

I carry their stories with me because I always believe you must know where you come from to know where you are going, especially if you want to do great things. Given the solid religious foundation set for me, I have learned one thing for sure: the importance of standing on the Word of God. In Jeremiah 29:11, God says, *"For I know the plans I have for you, plans to prosper you and give you hope for a future."* Early on, my parents made it clear that education would be a priority in my life. There were many other paths that I could have taken, but they made sure to keep me on the straight and narrow. Throughout my school years, this concept has remained a vital part of my being and has been the driving force behind my motivation to become a dentist. After graduating from Martin Luther King, Jr. Sr. High School in Detroit, Michigan, I was determined to attend an HBCU (Historically Black College or University). I attended Tennessee State University (TSU) in Nashville, Tennessee, for my undergraduate degree. Before I left, my cousin told me to enjoy going away to school because my college years would be some of the best years of my life. She told me to do my work and have as much fun as I could. So, I did. And she was right! There has never been another time like my college years. Once a year, I can relive snippets of that experience through my annual college homecoming visits.

While attending TSU, I was blessed with a good student advisor, Dr. Lois Harlston, who was pivotal in my career development. She taught me to always "fail forward," meaning, if you fail, do not get stuck in it. Find the positive and let it propel you forward. She also taught me the importance of being a trailblazer. While in school, our Health Sciences Department only had an organization for students interested in becoming physicians, SNMA (Student National Medical Association.) I asked Dr. Harlston if we could include something for students like me who were interested in dentistry. She replied, "Why don't you do the research and start it?" That statement guided me in establishing Tennessee State University's Undergraduate Student National Dental Association (USNDA) chapter. She left me with a quote by Ralph Emerson, "Do not follow where the path may lead, go instead where there is no path and leave a trail."

After graduating from Tennessee State University, I did a post-baccalaureate program at Meharry Medical College in Nashville, Tennessee. During my studies at Meharry College, I was introduced to the concept of health disparities. I became sensitive to all the health disparities and the need for health equity, but I never knew how this would all apply to dentistry. I used to write down my ideas when reading and studying my Bible. This is where I learned Habakkuk 2:2: *"And the Lord said write the vision and make it plain upon tables, that he may run that readeth it."* This verse is important even when you do not know how things will come together. Follow God's Word as He is the author of our lives, and He will make your path plain.

Next, I was accepted into Howard University's College of Dentistry in Washington, D.C. When I arrived, we were all sitting in the auditorium, and the Dean said, "I want you all to look around. You have all gotten here; that is the easy part…the hard part is getting out." I was like, what? I thought it was extremely hard just to get in. I encountered many financial and academic obstacles, but those hardships taught me perseverance. My mother would send me scriptures daily. She supported me emotionally, financially, and spiritually. I learned what it meant to truly rely on the word of God and to meditate on scriptures. I can recall when my refund check wasn't enough for that semester's last month of rent, and my parents didn't have the money to send me. I received a random call from our financial aid office informing me that I was awarded a $1,000 scholarship. I couldn't believe it! I kept saying, "I didn't apply for anything." The financial aid counselor said, "Just come down to the office. I have a check here with your name on it." I was so grateful and knew it was a gift from God as it was almost the exact amount I needed for my rent (DC living was expensive). I am a true believer that faith in God unlocks favor from God.

After graduating from Howard University, my dad wanted me to join the military. I was just not the "military" type of girl. I found two other options instead: The Department of Veteran Affairs and the U.S. Public Health Service Corps. Both programs assisted with loan repayment and had great retirement benefits. I applied to both programs and was accepted into a residency program at the John D. Dingell Department of Veteran Affairs Medical Center in Detroit (VAMC). It was great to come home, but there's nothing like going to school out of state and gaining that sense of independence. I completed my residency and had to take a board exam. I've never been good with standardized tests, so I failed the exam by one point. Disappointed with my exam results, I returned home to live with my mom. I was unable to work, so I went to the coffee shop daily to study. I started referring to it as "my office."

My normal "office" at Bigby Coffee was disrupted one day because their Wi-Fi was not working. My mom dropped me off at the Bigby Coffee near her church so I could continue my scheduled studies for that day. By this time, I was mentally exhausted and tired of my situation. I was drained from moping about my circumstances. I walked into Bigby and found a table near the front of the coffee shop. There was a lady who stared at me from the time I walked into the coffee shop. All I could think was, I must know her, and I just don't recognize her. She began to make me extremely uncomfortable with her stare. After 10-15 minutes, she approached my table and said, "You're pregnant." I looked at her as if she were crazy. I asked her with disgust, "What are you talking about?" She told me I was Pregnant in the Spirit and referred me to the book *Pregnant in the Spirit: Birth Life of Total Fulfillment -Your True Purpose by Princess Odilia*. She told me I was not there by accident, but God had led me to that location for a reason. I could only think of all the events that happened earlier that day, which led me to where I was at that very moment. She told me that I was on a journey. She said this was the easy part, and God was preparing me for the trials I had ahead. Again, I felt nothing could have gotten worse at the time than that situation. She told me what I was going through was preparing me for my purpose. At first, I thought she was crazy, but her prediction was accurate. I began crying in front of her and everyone else in the coffee shop. Then, I remembered the scripture, *"Do not neglect to show hospitality to strangers, for by doing so some have unwittingly entertained angels."* Hebrews 13:2 (NKJ)

Looking back on my life, I can see God's footprints carrying me along this journey. One must remember not to focus on their present circumstance. It is just one step on the journey that God has for your life to fulfill your purpose. After passing my board exam, I completed an Advanced Geriatric Fellowship at the Bruce W. Carter Miami Veteran Affairs Medical Center in Miami, Florida. This opportunity presented several trials of its own. Still, I overcame them as I blazed another trail, serving as the first Dentist among Physicians and Psychiatrists in the Program. *"My brethren, count it all joy when you come against various trials, knowing that the testing of your faith produces perseverance. Let perseverance finish its work so you may be mature and complete, not lacking anything."* James 1:2-4

Later, I was hired as a Research Investigator with the Geriatric Research and Education Clinical Center (GRECC) in the Miami VAMC. My focus areas were Health Disparities, Cultural Competence, and Health Equity. I gained valuable experience as a published researcher, educator, and clinician.

I currently serve as a Dental Director for our geriatric clinics in Atlanta, GA VAMC and as an Adjunct Assistant Professor of Medicine at Emory University. I serve as one of a handful of geriatric trained Hospital Dentists nationwide. All Glory to God!!! If this little Black girl from the CISC program at Martin Luther King Jr. Sr. High School can achieve goals she never even imagined, so can you!! As a woman of faith, God will give you strength to continue your journey. *"Commit to the Lord whatever you do, and He will establish your plans."* Proverbs 16:3.

Stand on the Word:

"Trust in the Lord with all your heart, lean not unto your own understanding, in all your ways acknowledge Him and He will direct your path." Proverbs 3:5,6

"I waited patiently on the Lord; and he inclined unto me, he heard my cry. He brought me up out of a horrible pit, out of the miry clay, and set my feet upon a rock, and established my goings. He hath put a new song in my mouth, even praise unto our God; many shall see it, and fear, and shall trust in the Lord." Psalm 40: 1-3

"But they that wait upon the Lord shall renew their strength; they shall mount up with wings as eagles; they shall run, and not be weary; and they shall walk, and not faint." Isaiah 40:31

Christie Hogue
Doctor of Dental Surgery (DDS)

Dr. Christie-Michele Hogue is a dental clinician, researcher, educator, and author. She has devoted over a decade of service to our nation's veterans as a dental clinician with the VAMC. She previously served as Dental Research Investigator at the Miami VA Geriatric Research Education and Clinical Center (GRECC). Dr. Hogue's research focuses on cultural competence and health literacy for minority veterans to address oral health disparities. Dr. Hogue's areas of interest include Oral Health and Frailty, Preventative/Behavioral Dentistry, Dental Ageism, Oral Health Literacy, Oral Health Disparities, Health Equity, and Cultural Competency. As a dental clinician, she is passionate about patient education and sharing the correlation between oral and systemic health. As a dental researcher, she hopes to enhance and innovate interactive models of care to empower patients to participate in their healthcare through knowledge and behavior modifications. She is the CEO and Founder of Mouth Mirrors LLC, an online education company, established to help bridge the gap through knowledge and education with an interdisciplinary approach to learning. The overall goal is to encourage health professionals to render compassionate, competent, comprehensive care for the oral health of our most vulnerable older populations. Dr. Hogue is also the host of the Aging Pearls Podcast. Dr. Hogue is a distinguished fellow of the American Geriatric Society. In 2023, Dr. Hogue was honored as one of the "Top 50 Women Leaders in Medicine."

Dr. Hogue completed an Advanced Fellowship in Geriatrics focusing on Geriatric Research, Education, and Clinic Care at Bruce W. Carter Miami VA. She completed her General Practice Residency (GPR) in her hometown of Detroit, Michigan at the John D. Dingell Veteran Affairs Medical Center. She graduated from Howard University College of Dentistry earning a Doctor of Dental Surgery (DDS). She completed her undergraduate studies at Tennessee State University graduating with a Bachelor of Science (BS).

QUESTIONS

1. **Influences and Role Models:** Dr. Hogue was influenced by her grandmother, father, and mother, each teaching her different life lessons. Reflect on the people who have significantly influenced your life. What key lessons have they taught you?

2. **Life as a Journey:** Dr. Hogue views life as a journey. How do you view your own life, and how does this perspective shape your goals and decisions?

3. **Overcoming Adversity:** Dr. Hogue faced various challenges in her academic and professional life. Think about a time you faced adversity. How did you overcome it, and what did you learn?

4. **Role of Faith:** Faith plays a significant role in Dr. Hogue's life and career. Discuss how personal beliefs or values have guided your choices and actions.

5. **The Power of Education:** Dr. Hogue's story emphasizes the importance of education in achieving goals. How has your educational journey influenced your life, and what are your future educational aspirations?

6. **Creating Opportunities:** Dr. Hogue started the USNDA chapter at her university. How can you take initiative in your environment to create opportunities for yourself and others?

7. **Embracing Unexpected Guidance:** Dr. Hogue's encounter at the coffee shop was pivotal. Have you ever received unexpected advice or guidance that significantly impacted your life?

8. **Resilience in the Face of Failure:** Dr. Hogue's experience with her board exams teaches resilience. How do you handle failure or setbacks, and what strategies do you use to move forward?

9. **Blazing Trails in Your Field:** Dr. Hogue was the first dentist in her fellowship program. How can you be a trailblazer in your chosen field or area of interest?

10. **Vision and Planning:** Dr. Hogue wrote down her ideas and planned for the future. How do you envision your future, and what steps are you taking to make your vision a reality?

Dr. LaShonda Fuller

"I will instruct you and teach you in the way you should go; I will guide you with My eye." Psalms 32:8

Hey, Magical Black Girl!

Before I share anything about my life, I need you to know that you were created with purpose. Your life matters to people who have never met you. The decisions you make do not just affect you but those who love you and those who will someday meet you.

When I was your age, I never imagined that my dreams and my commitment to school would provide me with the lifestyle and opportunities I have access to in my life right now. I dreamed a lot as a young girl. I prayed a lot. I wrote my thoughts down a lot as a teenager. Journaling was my friend. However, I recognized later in life that my initial dream as a young girl, to be a TV/Radio Broadcaster, was the beginning of the journey I would follow toward becoming a writer, counselor, professor and speaker. As a young girl, I loved talking. In elementary school, teachers always told my mother, "She gets her work done, but she talks a lot." Talking a lot in elementary school seemed like bad behavior when really talking was one of the gifts God gave me. Studying communications at Bowling Green University trained the natural talker in me to support my career as a writer, counselor, professor and speaker. Whatever you are dreaming about, keep dreaming. Your dreams will evolve, direct your path, and connect you to people who will support your dream development and achievement.

Dreams should serve as our guide of hope. A dream is an image in our minds that we believe we should be doing or something we desire to do with our lives.

Dreams give us insight into what we carry in our hearts, which is deeply felt. Just as we evolve from an adolescent to a teenager and a teenager to a young adult, our dreams also evolve. Whatever you feel passionate about early on in life, stick with the passion until the interest evolves over time. If your dreams happen to change, just know that every dream is a part of the process of you always coming into the future you.

Through my dreaming, praying, and writing, I was able to keep my goals and visions in front of me at each transition in life I experienced. Transitions that you, too, may experience may include graduating from high school and deciding if college or entering the workforce is the next direction. If college is the chosen life track, deciding on a major that would support your future life is a decision that should include prayer. Dreams cause us to have to make many decisions to achieve them. My older sister guided me, praying for God to direct my decisions. Use this book if you do not have a guide in your life. Including God in my decision-making about accomplishing my dreams has been my compass throughout life.

The attitude that supported me being successful away from family and close friends was an attitude of openness. Arriving in a new city, being open to meeting new people and challenging my ideals about life were moments that led me to pray even more. I needed help understanding the changes that were taking place around me and how it was necessary to respond in a way that would continue supporting my journey toward accomplishing my dreams. As an adult, I still pray about understanding transitional experiences that will help me succeed. Transitions in life are continuous and should not stop us from dreaming, but they will connect us to different people throughout life.

I managed to stay focused on my dreams by connecting with people who had experience in or worked in the area of my dreams. I joined specific activities and organizations that supported my dream and moved me closer to dream achievement. As a high school student, I listened to the teachers who particularly noticed me and said I was a scholar. Again, I would have never envisioned myself as a scholar, but someone else saw it and called the scholar out of me. When my teachers and mentors believed I would make a difference in the world, making a difference in the world became my priority. I wanted to make my parents, teachers, and mentors proud of me, which held me accountable to keep my dreams as my focus in life, but I also had a second priority. My second focus was to make it out of the lifestyle the hood supported while not forgetting what the hood taught me.

The hood taught me to trust no one and to focus on myself. The hood taught me that not everyone who looks like me is for me. The hood taught me that support is within the community. The hood taught me that pain is universal and creates resiliency if the pain is processed in a safe environment for understanding. The hood taught me there is glory in the struggle and that a little struggle "ain't bad." The hood taught me to work hard for what I love and whom I love. The hood taught me, "MY Black is Beautiful." The hood taught me not to be afraid but to take risks. Besides, what is there to lose? The hood taught me that not everyone will make it out, but when you do, because you will–you must make the best out of each opportunity until you trust yourself and the power within you. Then, you must return to the hood to spread the love but without being beaten up by the hood.

As a Mackenzie Stag Alum, early on in my learning experiences, I prioritized returning to my school and my hood to display what the hood produced in me. I wanted people to see how their psychological, emotional, or financial investment in me was paying off by sharing what I pursued while away at school. What was I doing with my time? Exploring life. Was I partying? Sure. Was I dating? Maybe. Was I going to class? Most often. Was I learning? Absolutely! I was learning about what worked for me as a young Black woman, what did not, and who could help me when life was not working. I wanted the hood to be proud of what I was becoming… a critical thinker.

I needed to share my experiences and tips on navigating this new world I was now a part of with those coming behind me. I called my return home when I would visit my old high school my community service. After leaving home for some time and visiting, I learned that some people will change and some will stay the same, but I must continue to change to become a better version of myself. Accept it.

To navigate the reality of friends and family changing or not, accepting my change was simply to remain open-minded, hopeful and true to my dreams. No one was able to help me manifest my dreams but me. Everything starts with self. Every decision will begin with you. Stay true to you.

Finally, as a Black woman from Detroit, my priority has always been to grow for myself first. Once I grew, I could bring resources back to my community to help others expand from poverty through the learned experiences that helped me grow. What I learned about the "learning experience" is that learning helps all people, even if not all people are open to learning. Nevertheless, learning something is not something we can keep to ourselves–sharing it with others is our responsibility. Therefore, what you learn throughout life that is useful and helps you move from one level of life to a higher level is for you to share with others. BUT share with those who are also committed to sharing with others who will continue to push the Black community out of poverty.

Let me be clear: poverty is a mindset, a way of thinking, not a way of being. To rise above poverty is to work. To work is to dream. To dream is to believe in the impossible. To believe in the impossible is to be hopeful. To be hopeful is to inspire. To inspire is to have a love for people. To have a love for people is to live a life of service. To live a life of service is to accept the idea that life is about growing to help others grow. Love you first. Then, love others the same way you love yourself, and life will bloom beyond your initial dreams. I promise.

Dr. LaShonda Fuller

Licensed Professional Counselor, National Certified Counselor
Author of *In Search for Love and Freedom* and Professor of Counseling

Dr. LaShonda Fuller is an accomplished Licensed Professional Counselor, National Certified Counselor, author, and professor of counseling. With a profound commitment to empowering young Black women, she leverages her extensive background in communications from Bowling Green State University to inspire through writing, counseling, and public speaking. Dr. Fuller's work emphasizes the importance of dreaming, personal growth, rest management, and community engagement, drawing from her own experiences to guide others. Her book, In Search for Love and Freedom, reflects her journey and the insights gained along the way. Dr. Fuller is dedicated to helping all people navigate life's transitions, advocating for mental health fostering resilience and hope globally.

QUESTIONS

1. **Purpose and Influence:** Dr. Fuller emphasizes the importance of understanding one's purpose and the impact of our decisions on others. Reflecting on Dr. Fuller's insights, how do you see your own purpose, and in what ways do you think your decisions are influencing both your life and those around you?

2. **Evolution of Dreams:** Dr. Fuller's aspirations transitioned from a young girl dreaming of TV/Radio Broadcasting to her successful roles as a writer, counselor, professor, and speaker. Reflect on how your own dreams have evolved over time. What influenced these changes, and how does Dr. Fuller's journey inspire you to pursue your evolving dreams?

3. **The Role of Journaling:** Journaling was a critical tool for Dr. Fuller in understanding and achieving her dreams. Have you ever used journaling or another method to navigate your dreams and decisions? Discuss how this approach has helped you in clarifying your goals and path.

4. **Guidance and Decision Making:** The guidance from her sister and her faith played a significant role in Dr. Fuller's decision-making. Who or what provides you with similar guidance when faced with significant life decisions, and how has this shaped your journey?

5. **Openness to Change and Transition:** Dr. Fuller credits her success to maintaining an openness to new experiences and transitions. Share a moment when you had to be open to change or a new chapter in your life. What did you learn from this experience, and how did it contribute to your personal growth?

6. **Seeking and Finding Support:** Finding supportive individuals was crucial for Dr. Fuller in achieving her dreams. Reflect on how you seek support for your ambitions. Can you share a time when the support from someone else was pivotal in your pursuit of a goal?

7. **Lessons from the Hood:** Dr. Fuller draws valuable lessons from her upbringing. What lessons have you learned from your own environment or community, and how have these insights shaped your perspective on life and success?

8. **Returning and Giving Back:** Dr. Fuller emphasizes the importance of giving back to her community. How do you plan to give back to your community or another group that has been instrumental in your life? Why is this act of giving back significant to you?

9. **The Importance of Learning and Sharing Knowledge:** Dr. Fuller believes in the power of learning and the responsibility to share that knowledge with others. What is a key lesson or piece of knowledge you've acquired that you feel is important to share? How do you intend to pass this knowledge on?

10. **Overcoming the Poverty Mindset:** Dr. Fuller discusses overcoming a mindset of poverty to achieve success. How are you working to overcome challenges and perceived limitations in your own life? How can Dr. Fuller's perspective inspire you to push beyond these boundaries?

Joslyn Shannon-Harmon, Ph.D.

"God will do abundantly, above and beyond all that you could ask for or think." Ephesians 3:20

My name is Joslyn Shannon-Harmon, and I must say my God has spoiled me. Everything that I have ever hoped and wanted for, He has provided. However, these blessings often did not come when I wanted them to, and I have often experienced setbacks (many of my own doing). But regardless of getting in my own way, God went above and beyond all I could ask for. He made a way out of no way. He showed up and showed out!

I was educated in the Detroit Public School System from 1st through 12th grade. I attended Duffield Elementary School, Whitney Young Middle School, and the prestigious Dr. Martin Luther King, Jr. Senior High School. There was nothing I wanted more at the end of my middle school years than to be accepted to King. My parents graduated from Eastern High School (the former name of King High School), my aunts and uncles had gone there, and I already had many friends and family there. When I got the news I was accepted to King, I was elated. But at the time, I did not know how this high school experience would shape my life. My high school years were really some of the best years of my life. I gained lifelong friends and had experiences I will never forget. One experience stands out amongst the others because it reflects on God's word of doing abundantly, above and beyond all that I could ask for, which really set my motivation in life.

During my senior year at King High School, I was determined to improve my grades to make it into the National Honor Society. When the first report cards came out, I was one grade short of having the grade point average to qualify for the honor society. I confronted the teacher that I believed was holding me back from my goal. I even had my mother come to the school for a conference. In the conference, my teacher showed my mother my work compared to my classmates' work. I had met the requirements, but as she stated, "I did not go above and beyond the call of duty." My mother agreed, and I had to keep that grade, preventing me from being on the National Honor Society. I was upset with that teacher for a long time; however, her words resonated with me: "Go above and beyond the call of duty." I began working hard to show this teacher I wasn't mediocre. I soon became one of her best students. At the end of the school year, I finally got the grade I set out to achieve, but it was too late for the National Honor Society. However, this is not where the story ends.

As I continued on to college, I lived by those words: "Go above and beyond the call of duty." I became pregnant with my first child during my first year in college. I heard so many comments in my face and behind my back about how I ruined my life and became a statistic. I used these comments to add "fuel to my fire." I worked hard to go above and beyond the call of duty and I graduated with a Bachelor's in Business Administration from Central Michigan University in three years, despite my setbacks.

I pursued a Master of Business Administration (MBA) degree, but before I finished, I decided to try teaching. My first teaching interview was at Osborn High School, and to my surprise, who was there to receive my resume and possibly hire me? The same teacher who told me to go above and beyond the call of duty. I was so glad that I had mended my relationship with her because If I hadn't, I might not have had favor. I got the job, but since I didn't major in education, I had to go back to school to get a teaching certificate. As I mentioned before, I was already working on an MBA, so after finishing that, I worked on my teaching certificate. The timing was perfect because when I finished my MBA at Davenport University, the University of Detroit Mercy had just started a three-year program (at a discounted price) where I could get a teaching certificate in two areas and a Master of Arts in Teaching at the same time.

God showed up and showed out throughout my time at the University of Detroit Mercy. He made a way for me to get books when I couldn't afford them. He provided me with a great support network to watch my son while I was taking classes and gave me a mind to fix what I messed up. One particular time stands out. One day, I decided to miss class. When I talked to my classmates, they told me we had a big assignment, and anyone who signed up to go first received extra points. Because I didn't attend class, I missed the opportunity to sign up and receive the much-needed extra points. But God put something on my heart and in my head. He told me to do the project, go above and beyond, be ready to present it on the first day and get to class early. I got to class early and explained to my teacher that I missed the sign-up day and that if anyone who signed up to present that day wasn't ready, I was. Luckily one of the people due to present was not ready, and I was able to move into their spot to present and receive the extra points. God had again done abundantly, above and beyond all I could imagine.

Not long after that, an extraordinary opportunity presented itself at the University of Detroit Mercy. I got the chance to study abroad in Italy, and I still maintained a 3.9 grade point average. This grade point average allowed me to be accepted into the Jesuit Honor Society. So, although I did not meet the requirements for the National Honor Society in high school, I exceeded the requirements for the Honor Society in college. God showed me again He would do abundantly, above and beyond all I could ask for and think.

I completed my program at the University of Detroit Mercy in three years, which allowed me to have a Bachelor's degree, two Master's degrees and two teaching certifications (special education and business education).

After seven years at Osborn High School, I started teaching at Central High School. After teaching at Central High School for two years, I returned to my alma mater, King High School, as a teacher. During this time, I was accepted into the Doctorate of Education program at Wayne State University. I quickly moved through the courses of this program, but life happened, and I could not complete my degree at the time.

After teaching for two years at King High School, I got married, moved to Dallas, Texas, and had another child. I continued my teaching career at Woodrow Wilson High School in the Dallas Independent School District (DISD). Later, I began teaching at Wilmer-Hutchins High School in DISD. The entire time I was teaching in Dallas, I had my eye on becoming an assistant principal or principal. I applied for many school leadership positions but didn't get them. I was told in Dallas, you have to know somebody to move up. Finally, a friend encouraged me to apply for a central office leadership position, and I got it without knowing anyone but God. I came to Dallas with the mentality of going above and beyond the call of duty, so God did abundantly, above and beyond all I could imagine. I had only worked in Dallas for a year and a few months and was already receiving a promotion.

While working in the central office, God aligned me with people who helped prepare me for greater things. I had my eyes on becoming a supervisor. However, shortly after trying to secure that promotion, I became pregnant with my third child. This time, the timing wasn't so great. Although they aren't supposed to, many companies will not hire or promote a pregnant woman because of the time off they will need when they give birth to their baby. But yet again, God showed up and did abundantly, above and beyond. I got the job and became a special education supervisor for the DISD.

After a few years of being the supervisor, COVID happened. While COVID was horrible, some good things came from it. Wayne State University (the school I attended while working on my doctorate) broadened their perspective and was forced to do more distance learning than in person. There was a push to assist students in completing degrees. My advisor reached out to me and said let's get this done. The only caveat was that I was in a Ph.D. program, but because so much time passed, I had to complete it with an Ed.D. This was a hard pill to swallow, but It was better to have a completed Ed.D. than an incomplete Ph.D. My advisor at Wayne State University worked with me virtually to guide me into finishing. None of this could have happened without God doing abundantly above and beyond all I could want and think.

As you can see, God has shown up and shown out throughout my life. I'd say I turned out pretty well for a young Black girl from the City of Detroit who attended Detroit Public Schools. However, without God, the foundation I received early on in Detroit Public Schools, and the push from my high school teacher, my drive and determination would've looked much different. Many times, I got in my own way. The blessings and favor often didn't come when I wanted them to. However, as the old saying goes, He's an on-time God. I will continue to live by the motto of going above and beyond the call of duty. As long as I believe in God, He has and will continue to do abundantly, above and beyond all I can ask for and think.

Joslyn Shannon-Harmon, Ph.D.

Dr. Joslyn Shannon-Harmon is a distinguished education professional with a rich, non-traditional background that spans a broad spectrum of skills, including training and professional development, diversity and inclusion, and project management. She has trained over 10,000 individuals and fostered partnerships across educational institutions, workforce agencies, and corporations. Harmon has excelled in developing impactful programs, maintaining federal compliance, and managing significant budgets, highlighting her leadership and innovative capabilities. Her journey, marked by perseverance and faith, led her from the Detroit Public School System to achieving multiple degrees and certifications. Harmon's story is one of overcoming obstacles, driven by a belief in going "above and beyond the call of duty," a principle that has guided her through personal challenges and professional achievements alike.

QUESTIONS

1. **Embracing Setbacks:** Dr. Joslyn Shannon-Harmon shares how setbacks, many of her own doing, did not deter her from achieving her dreams. Reflect on a setback you have encountered in your life. How did you overcome it, and what did you learn about perseverance and faith through that experience?

2. **The Influence of High School:** Dr. Joslyn's time at Dr. Martin Luther King, Jr. Senior High School had a profound impact on her life. Think about your own high school experience. How did it shape your motivations and aspirations for the future?

3. **Striving for Excellence:** Despite initially being denied entry into the National Honor Society, Dr. Joslyn used the feedback to motivate herself to go "above and beyond the call of duty." Recall a time when you were motivated by criticism or rejection. How did it fuel your desire to excel, and what was the outcome?

4. **Balancing Responsibilities:** As a college student and a new mother, Dr. Joslyn graduated with a Bachelor's in Business Administration in three years. Discuss a period in your life when you had to balance multiple responsibilities. How did you manage, and what strategies helped you succeed?

5. **The Role of Educators:** Dr. Joslyn's relationship with a former teacher, who once challenged her, later played a pivotal role in her career path. Describe an educator who has made a significant impact on your life. How did their guidance or challenge influence your personal or professional journey?

6. **God's Timing:** Dr. Joslyn attributes her success to her faith and God's timing, emphasizing that blessings often come not when we want them but when we need them. Share a moment in your life when you felt that timing played a crucial role in receiving a blessing or opportunity.

7. **The Power of Determination:** Despite the skepticism she faced, Dr. Joslyn achieved remarkable academic and professional success. Reflect on a goal you achieved against the odds. What drove you to keep going, and how did you prove doubters wrong?

8. **Giving Back and Mentorship:** Dr Joslyn's journey from student to educator in the Detroit Public School system highlights the importance of giving back. How do you plan to or how have you given back to your community or alma mater? Why is this important to you?

9. **Adapting to Life Changes:** Moving to Dallas and facing new challenges, Dr. Joslyn continued to advance her career and education. Discuss a significant life change you have experienced. How did you adapt, and what lessons did you learn about resilience and faith?

10. **The Importance of a Support System:** Throughout her journey, Dr. Joslyn highlights the importance of having a support system, including God, family, and mentors. Reflect on your support system. How has it helped you navigate challenges and achieve your goals?

Dr. Sonya Franklin Burney

"Each of you should use whatever gift you have received to serve others, as faithful stewards of God's grace in its various forms." 1 Peter 4:10

Tradition, excellence, scholarship and pride are a few words that come to mind when I think about my alma mater, Cass Technical High School. Attending Cass Tech and playing on the basketball team has been a tradition in my family that has been passed down over generations. My father and two older brothers played varsity basketball and graduated from Cass Tech. Growing up, I dreamed of going to Cass Tech and playing on the basketball team. Our family tradition was passed on to two of my nephews, who also graduated and played varsity basketball. Attending and graduating from Cass Tech has been a tradition of many Detroit families. Personally, it was more than just playing basketball for me; it was also the academics that were important. From the stories my father shared, I learned that some of the brightest and most successful people from Detroit graduated from Cass Tech.

Academically, I knew that Cass was one of the top schools in Michigan. The grading scale alone showcased that Cass Tech was not a school to take lightly. It was as follows: 100% - 92% = A, 91% - 82% = B, 81% - 72% = C, 71% - 62 =D, 61% - below = F. When I realized a 91% was a B at Cass, I knew I would have to work harder than I did in middle school. This was only the beginning of many adjustments.

The first two years of high school as a student athlete were filled with discovery and exploration. Playing high school basketball at a Division I school, I felt a little intimidated because almost everyone on the team played at a high level, which made it harder to stand out as a skilled player. After being a part of the starting five lineup since the beginning of my basketball career, I had to adjust to coming off the bench. The transition to high school was eased by finding a community within the girls' basketball team. I developed a strong relationship with three young women, who gave me a strong foundation of true friendship and taught me how to be a good friend. We spent much time together, both on and off the court. We often hung out at each other's houses, the mall, or Taco Bell and Coney Island. My friend group supported me through all the many challenges of my teenage years. They taught me what it meant to truly have your girl's back!

Academically, the biggest adjustment was learning how to work hard to meet and exceed the teachers' expectations. I quickly discovered that many teachers at Cass Tech had high expectations of me as a student. They pushed me to work hard and produce excellent work. My 10th-grade English teacher, Ms. Williams, was one of the most memorable teachers I had in high school. Her room was filled with posters of African Kings and Queens, some we never even heard of before. She walked with her head high, wearing traditional African attire with a matching head wrap every single day.

I once recall my class receiving harsh feedback on a writing assignment. Ms. Williams was not happy with our lack of attention to proper grammar. The next day, she angrily taught a week-long lesson on verbs and nouns. She even tested us on it the following week to make sure the class knew the material. This showed me that mediocrity should never be an option and that I should always strive for excellence. All of my English teachers from 9th through 12th grade at Cass somehow left a lasting impression on me. From extensive grammar lessons to feedback on rewriting a paper I thought was an A+, I learned many valuable lessons. My teachers showed me how to articulate my written thoughts in a well-thought-out and organized format.

My 11th-grade year might have been the most challenging socially and academically. I was no longer on the basketball team and struggled to find my purpose and identity without playing varsity basketball. I felt a sense of disappointment in myself and my ability to succeed. I then began to notice an impact on my academics. I knew something had to change. I had to rediscover myself and work to find out who I wanted to become. I began working with the school social worker as a student aid, allowing me to engage in a different extracurricular activity besides basketball. I also began to step up my efforts in school by working harder in classes. I would come to class early to put math homework problems on the board for extra credit and received additional help from my Spanish teacher during lunch. By the end of the school year, I was back on track and ready to continue on my path to academic achievement.

By my senior year in high school, I had gained more confidence academically. I also got a part-time job after school, which would not have been possible if I were playing varsity basketball. Senior year was when I began to appreciate the amazing teachers I came across, in addition to enjoying my high school experience the most. I was starting to be interested in becoming a teacher; however, my interest was sparked by the not-so-great teachers in high school. Those mediocre teachers inspired me with the desire to be an advocate for students. This is where my interest in education was born. I graduated from Cass Tech with honors and attended Eastern Michigan University that fall, known for its excellent education program.

In high school, I connected with teachers who showed respect, care, and compassion for me and my peers. In my eyes, that is what support looked and felt like. I knew I wanted to do something in education; however, the only career path that came to mind was a teacher. I wanted to provide a voice for the youth, but I was unsure if becoming a secondary teacher was the route I wanted to take. I went to college to pursue a secondary teaching degree. That plan changed when I discovered it took an average of 5 years to complete the certification. I then decided to major in business, which was much harder than anticipated. After struggling through statistics, finance, and production operations management (I am still not sure what that class was) classes, I graduated with a Bachelor of Business Administration degree from Eastern Michigan University in 4 ½ years.

The year I graduated from college, finding a job in my field was difficult due to the impact of 9/11, so I worked in multiple industries until I found my match. While in college, I worked at Walmart as a manager and continued working there for several months after graduation. In an attempt to work closer to home, I took an unpaid internship with the Detroit Pistons working in Sales. I also worked as a manager at a clothing store. After working there for one season, I worked at a car rental company. Working long hours and pay in entry level jobs helped me discover very quickly that the corporate environment was not one I thrived in as a professional. Several years after completing my undergraduate degree and working unfulfilling jobs, I began exploring graduate programs. At the time, I was working at a proprietary for-profit college and also looking to work at a large university. After months of searching, I obtained a job at the University of Michigan (UM). After two years of working at UM, I went back to Eastern Michigan University and obtained a Master's degree in Higher Education and Student Affairs. After completing my Master's degree and working as an academic advisor, I decided to move into a leadership role. I felt most successful leaders in higher education had a doctoral degree, so I enrolled in the Doctor of Philosophy in Educational Leadership program at Eastern Michigan while working full-time and raising a young family. It took me six years to complete the program. I could not have done it without the support of my husband, close friends, and supportive faculty.

As a professional at the midpoint of my career, I have spent most of my 20-year career working as a higher education practitioner in Academic Advising Centers, developing Academic Success Programs, and managing College Access & Transition Programs. It took me years to learn that my source of energy and passion as a professional is centered around overall well-being and working in an environment that is flexible and better aligned with my purpose and natural talents and gifts. Today, I work in the non-profit sector as a director, helping to build organizational wellness and structure while focusing on staff development and organizational sustainability. In addition, I own Essence 4 Success Consulting, a coaching and consulting company supporting undergraduate, graduate, and Ph.D. students through their educational journey. I have a true purpose and gift to provide coaching and consulting to students of color, just like Detroit Public School (DPS) alumni who regularly fight against the stigma of being an underrepresented scholar in a Predominately White Institution (PWI), in addition to fighting the historical inequities of students of color in an academic setting.

As a Cass Tech graduate, I have always felt pride. As a Detroit Public School (DPS) alumni, I hold my head high. Attending DPS from elementary through high school gave me the resilience needed to work hard and excel. I was surrounded by like-minded students and guided by strong teachers and administrators who wanted us to succeed. I am proud to say that I am from Detroit, graduated from Cass Tech, and have a PhD! I am truly a success story that can inspire DPS students. To all my fellow DPS students, know that you are magical, and you, too, can be an inspiration to others. You can obtain any career or lifestyle you desire with hard work and discipline. If you are unsatisfied with an outcome, do something different, and don't be afraid to try new things. Work to connect with others and build relationships. Those connections may someday be a resource and blessing to you. Discover your true gifts and talents and give back.

Dr. Sonya Franklin Burney

Dr. Sonya Franklin Burney was born and raised in Detroit, Michigan. She studied both instrumental and vocal music, eventually acquiring summer camp scholarships to attend The Blue Lake Fine Arts Camp and Interlochen Fine Arts Camp.

While attending Cass Technical High School, Sonya was a music major and performed in numerous bands and vocal ensembles: Symphony Band, The Madrigals, along with the prestigious and nationally-known Harp and Vocal Ensemble. She also made history in the existence of the school when she became one of two first drum majors of Cass Tech's first-ever marching band. During this time, she studied under the premiere instruction of Mrs. Patricia Terry-Ross, Mr. Dalos Grobe, and the late band maestro, Mr. Benjamin L. Pruitt. In her senior year, Sonya earned a four-year merit scholarship to The University of Michigan's School of Music.

Sonya studied voice with Professor Emeritus George Shirley, former tenor with the New York Metropolitan Opera, and recent Presidential Medal of Freedom Award from President Obama in 2016. She also studied chorus and conducting under the baton of Dr. Jerry Blackstone. She also sang with Mr. Brazeal Dennard, founder of The Brazeal Dennard Chorale of Detroit, who gave her the opportunity to sing for the late opera great Mr. William Warfield and famed pianist, the late Ms. Sylvia Olden Lee.

After graduating with two undergraduate degrees in English and Voice Performance from The University of Michigan, Sonya moved to California to perform with Dr. Albert McNeil and the world-renowned Albert McNeil Jubilee Singers of Los Angeles. She was able to hone her soloing and performing skills in the United States, Canada, Europe and South America as a featured soloist and traveling member singing in prestigious halls such as Carnegie Hall in New York City. During her time in California, she also worked with Wynton Marsalis for the Warner Bros. movie, "Rosewood." Other operatic roles include the late Marian Anderson at Middle Tennessee State University, Virginia Creeper with The Nashville Opera, and as a featured soloist while performing with The Nashville Symphony Chorus and the Grammy-award winning Nashville Symphony Orchestra.

As an editor, copyeditor, writer, speaker, and company trainer of publications nationwide, Sonya has served with worldwide companies such as Alfred Music Publishing Inc., as well as The Sunday School Publishing Board of the National Baptist Convention, USA, Inc. Because of her many accomplishments, Sonya was recommended by her Alpha Kappa Alpha sorority chapter members to be an ATHENA nominee for women in service and leadership to the Nashville, Tennessee community in 2011.

As a published author, Sonya published her first book Young Warren Sings! in 2004. This book later premiered as a stage play. She has written other various publications and books for nationwide publishers. Her latest, "Living Beneath" premiered in 2019 addressing caregiver roles, family relationships and wealth when family members are impacted with dementia and Alzheimer diseases.

As an educator since 2011, Sonya has been a trained and certified teacher in the classroom at the secondary and collegiate levels. While teaching and performing numerous leadership roles in school organizations, she completed her doctorate in Educational Leadership in 2017. Sonya currently resides in a north suburb of Atlanta, Georgia and continues to move in her gifts.

QUESTIONS

1. **Tradition and Family Influence:** Dr. Sonya Franklin Burney discusses the significance of her family's tradition of attending Cass Technical High School and their involvement in sports. Reflect on a family tradition that has influenced your choices in education or career. How has this tradition shaped your goals?

2. **Academic Challenges and Self-Improvement:** Realizing the competitive environment at Cass Tech, Dr. Franklin Burney was determined to elevate her academic performance. Describe a time when you had to push beyond your limits academically. What motivated you, and how did you achieve your goals?

3. **Identity Beyond Athletics:** After stepping away from basketball, Dr. Franklin Burney faced challenges in redefining her identity. Share a moment when an external change forced you to rediscover who you are. What did you learn about yourself in the process?

4. **Exploring Career Paths:** Dr. Franklin Burney's journey through various jobs before finding her calling highlights the value of exploration. Discuss a period in your life when you were exploring different career or educational paths. How did these experiences contribute to finding your passion?

5. **Resilience and Support Networks:** The importance of resilience and a strong support network is a central theme in Dr. Franklin Burney's story. Reflect on how your support network has helped you face a significant challenge. Who are the key figures, and what role did they play?

6. **The Role of Mentors:** Dr. Franklin Burney mentions the influence of mentors in her personal and professional development. Think about a mentor in your life. How have they guided you, and what impact has this relationship had on your journey?

7. **The Impact of Service and Community Engagement:** Her work in the non-profit sector underscores Dr. Franklin Burney's commitment to service. Reflect on a time when you engaged with your community or performed service. What did you learn, and how has it influenced your perspective on success?

8. **Lifelong Learning and Adaptability:** Dr. Franklin Burney's educational pursuits demonstrate her belief in lifelong learning. Discuss a skill or subject you've recently begun learning or wish to learn. Why is this important to you, and how do you plan to incorporate this learning into your life?

9. **Overcoming Prejudice and Advocating for Equity:** Addressing and overcoming societal challenges is an underlying theme in Dr. Franklin Burney's career. Share an instance when you encountered prejudice or inequity. How did you respond, and what did you learn from the experience?

10. **Vision for the Future and Legacy:** Dr. Franklin Burney is motivated by a desire to leave a lasting impact. Envision the legacy you wish to leave in your community or field. What steps are you taking to achieve this, and how does your vision inspire your daily actions?

Dr. Kali Keller, PT, DPT, CLT-LANA

"Do not be anxious about anything, but in every situation, by prayer and petition, with thanksgiving, present your requests to God." Philippians 4:6

My childhood was pretty unremarkable until fourth grade. Unbeknownst to me, my mother and our neighbor, Mrs. Jackson, discussed my education. Mrs. Jackson's daughter, Tiffany, also attended St. Benedict Catholic School, which I attended until 3rd grade, but had to leave due to financial hardship. Mrs. Jackson asked what schools my mom intended for me to go to, and my mother simply replied that I would just attend the neighborhood schools, which were John R. King Elementary, Cerveny Middle School and Cooley High School. For those who don't know, including my mom at the time, these particular schools were notorious in the city of Detroit for fighting, gang activity and occasional weapons being brought on the schools' campuses by students. Once my mother learned about these extracurricular activities, she worked on figuring out a way to get me into better schools.

Randomly, and shortly after my mom's conversation with Mrs. Jackson, my mother ran into one of her favorite grade school teachers during the summer before I entered fourth grade, and she brought up her quest for finding better school options for me that she could afford. My mom's teacher told her that Bates Academy was a great school for the gifted and talented. The catch was that you needed to test to get in, and the deadline for testing for the upcoming semester had passed, but she would see what she could do. About a week after my first week of fourth grade at King Elementary, my mom received a letter stating I had been accepted to Bates Academy. And that was when my educational journey changed courses.

Going to Bates Academy was intimidating, to say the least. Before this, I was the smartest kid in the class; now, I was amongst kids who were just as smart and even smarter than me. I was surrounded by kids who strived to do better instead of being "too cool" to excel. My homework went from simple arithmetic to academic games and vocabulary spelling words to vocabulary skill building (VSB) words that would begin to shape my evolved relationship with words. At the young age of 10, I began discussing which college I would attend, something that was never brought up nor did I even think of considering. At Bates Academy, we were taught to celebrate and be proud of our Black history. We were exposed to the arts and advanced mathematics and constantly challenged to go above and beyond the status quo. I attended Bates Academy from 4th to 8th grade. By the time I graduated, I was convinced I could've been prepared for my first year at any university, let alone high school. But high school was the inevitable next step, and there were only three choices: Cass, King, or Renaissance. I chose Cass Tech and became a mighty, mighty Technician.

Outside of school, my mom kept me busy with the arts. I took art classes and music lessons, but what I loved the most were my dance classes. My mother put me in my first dance class at the age of three and saw an innate talent in me, so much so that she enrolled me in dance classes at the Center for Creative Studies, where I took ballet and African dance classes. I picked up on my African dance lessons quickly, and I believe it was because of an unexplained ancestral and spiritual connection with the drums. My dad was running late one day to pick me up after class, and I distinctly remember the next level of dancers coming in, putting on these satin slippers and dancing on their toes. I went home that day and told my parents I wanted to dance on my toes, too!

A few years later, the American Ballet Theater was holding auditions for their summer intensive program. At that time, I knew I was good enough. I mean, I was one of the top dancers in my class. When I arrived at the audition, I was the only "one" and immediately became self-conscious. My mom encouraged me to finish the audition, which was completely over my head. I did not know the terminology, could barely pick up the choreography, and I was the only Black girl in the building and was completely embarrassed. I remember wanting to leave, but my mom encouraged me to stay for the whole thing.

After the terrifying event, we went to get ice cream, and later that night, I was determined to find better dance classes. O'Day School of Dance would be where I would fine-tune my technique, presentation and performance skills. I excelled and became one of the principal dancers of the Detroit Ballet Theatre by the age of 16. In addition, just days before graduating from high school, I was reaching new heights with my dancing. I was one of three dancers selected amongst nearly 200 to join the Detroit Pistons' Automotion Dance Team, the youngest ever to join the team.

My senior year was filled with difficult decisions to make. Attending college at either of the prestigious schools majoring in engineering was a proud moment for my family. I had been accepted to both schools I applied to: Hampton University in Hampton, Virginia, and Michigan State University in Lansing, Michigan. I also auditioned for the Dance Theater of Harlem just a year prior and was one of their top picks to perform at the Fox Theatre during their stay in Detroit. To add to all that, I was trying to balance all this while having my first serious boyfriend. The pressure was so overwhelming. I decided to go to Michigan State University. I could make my parents proud, stay close to my boyfriend and dance with the Pistons' Automotion Dance Team. This was truly one of the hardest decisions I have made in my life, and even to this day, one of my greatest regrets was basing my decision solely on trying to appease my loved ones instead of following my heart. But everything happens for a reason.

My four and a half years at Michigan State University were amazing, but many changes came with it. I broke up with my boyfriend and realized the commute back and forth from campus to the Palace of Auburn Hills became too much to bear. I eventually had to quit the dance team. But I auditioned and made the Michigan State Motion Dance Team, and all was well with the world again. I also took advantage of a program to study abroad in Australia. I got my first passport and spent two months exploring a new world filled with kangaroos and crocodiles. One of the most devastating losses I had to endure through it all was losing my father.

After a few internships with General Motors, I also began to realize that engineering was not the career for me and was contemplating switching majors, but an advisor in the School of Engineering tried to discourage me from auditioning for the MSU Dance Team saying that I would not be able to balance both and I had to prove her wrong.

During my senior year in college, I had the misfortune of tearing my ACL during one of our dance rehearsals. By the time I got the diagnosis, I was no longer on my parents' health insurance. This was devastating because I finally decided to pursue my dance career after I graduated college. In December, I graduated with my Bachelor of Science in Engineering. Though it was a proud moment in my life, I wondered how this injury impacted my plans to finally pursue the dance career I longed for.

I started working at an automotive supplier doing marketing back in Detroit. It was a lackluster position, but the biggest highlight was my health insurance plan, which had no provisions for pre-existing conditions. When I realized that, I found one of the best orthopedic surgeons in the Detroit metropolitan area and arranged to have my ACL reconstructed. Three months after I finished my physical therapy, I was called into the HR office and was told the company was going out of business, and I was one of the first to be laid off.

I had vowed that if I could get my knee fixed, I would finally pursue my dance career. The following year, I did just that. In April of the following year, I drove 2,300 miles from Detroit to L.A., where I would start my new life as a professional dancer. I obtained a dance agent and began the brutal life as a struggling artist.

I found a stable "day job" as a legal assistant in the legal department at Paramount Pictures in Hollywood and did a decent job balancing work with auditions. Over the time spent in L.A. I managed to build a decent resume, including working with Disney and Royal Caribbean and becoming the 2012 World Latin Dance Cup Champion for Cha-Cha. Despite my successes, I found this lifestyle somewhat pointless and began researching other career options.

The turning point happened when my mom was diagnosed with non-Hodgkin's lymphoma amid my desire for a career change. This was life-altering because when she returned home from the hospital, she was incredibly weak and could barely walk. To help my mom regain her strength, I returned home and showed her a few exercises I had learned from my many physical therapy sessions. It was challenging, but I helped my mom regain her strength. At that point, I decided I would become a physical therapist.

I returned to L.A. and enrolled in night classes at The University of California Los Angeles (UCLA) to fulfill my prerequisites to attend physical therapy school. I applied to only one school, Washington University School of Medicine in St. Louis, Missouri and graduated to become a Doctor of Physical Therapy.

I currently treat patients for common injuries related to the back, knee, shoulder, etc., but I also specialize in cancer rehabilitation and lymphedema therapy, which is a combination of physical therapy and garments or bandaging that moves fluid from areas affected by lymphedema in which I help patients restore their strength, function and quality of life. In addition to that, I treat performing artists recovering from dance injuries and reduce the risk of injuries to optimize their performance lifespan.

All in all, I have lived an unconventional life, to say the least, but the pivotal moment happened when my mom decided to get me into the best public schools in Detroit, and I am forever grateful for that.

Dr. Kali Keller, PT, DPT, CLT-LANA

Kali Keller is a Doctor of Physical Therapy, LANA-certified lymphedema therapist, and cancer rehabilitation specialist. Originating from a profound passion for dance, her career evolved significantly after aiding in her mother's recovery from non-Hodgkin's lymphoma. This pivotal moment redirected her focus towards physical therapy, leading her to specialize in cancer rehabilitation and the treatment of performing artists. Dr. Keller, an alumna of Washington University School of Medicine in St. Louis, Missouri, is dedicated to restoring movement, function, and quality of life for her patients, with a special focus on injury prevention and optimizing performance longevity for artists.

QUESTIONS

1. **Unexpected Opportunities and Change:** Dr. Kali Keller's journey took a pivotal turn due to her mother's conversation with a former teacher, leading to her acceptance into Bates Academy. Reflect on a time when an unexpected opportunity came your way. How did it change your educational or career path, and what impact did it have on your future aspirations?

2. **Academic and Social Challenges:** Transitioning to Bates Academy introduced Dr. Keller to a more competitive academic environment and a new peer group. Think about a time when you faced challenges after a significant change in your life. How did you adapt to this new environment, and what lessons did you learn about yourself?

3. **The Power of Arts in Personal Growth:** Dr. Keller's involvement in dance from a young age played a crucial role in her personal development. Discuss how participating in the arts or a particular hobby has influenced your growth. What skills or lessons did you gain from this experience?

4. **Overcoming Self-Doubt and External Perceptions:** The audition for the American Ballet Theater was a challenging experience for Dr. Keller, making her feel out of place and self-conscious. Share a moment when you felt overwhelmed by self-doubt or judged by others. How did you overcome these feelings, and what did the experience teach you?

5. **Decision Making and Regrets:** Choosing Michigan State University over pursuing her dance career was a decision Dr. Keller described as one of her greatest regrets. Reflect on a significant decision you've made in your life. Do you have any regrets, and what did you learn from making that choice?

6. **Navigating Loss and Change:** The loss of Dr. Keller's father during her time at Michigan State University was a significant emotional challenge. Describe a loss or significant change you have experienced. How did it affect you, and how did you find strength to move forward?

7. **Career Exploration and Shifts:** Initially pursuing engineering, Dr. Keller realized it wasn't her passion and eventually found her calling in physical therapy. Have you ever experienced a shift in your career or educational focus? What prompted the change, and how did you navigate the transition?

8. **Turning Points and New Directions:** The diagnosis and recovery of Dr. Keller's mother from non-Hodgkin's lymphoma was a turning point in her life, leading her to pursue a career in physical therapy. Discuss a turning point in your life that led you to discover a new passion or career path. How did this moment redefine your goals and aspirations?

9. **Impact of Physical Therapy on Life:** Specializing in cancer rehabilitation and lymphedema therapy, Dr. Keller has been able to make a significant impact on her patients' lives. Reflect on a time when helping someone else also led to your own personal growth or a deeper understanding of your purpose.

10. **Reflecting on Life's Unconventional Journeys:** Dr. Keller views her life as unconventional but pivotal moments, such as changing schools, have shaped her into who she is. Consider the unconventional aspects of your own journey. How have these moments shaped your identity and perspective on life?

Aina N. Watkins, BBA, JD, LLM.

"But the Lord said to Samuel, "Do not consider his appearance or his height, for I have rejected him. The Lord does not look at the things people look at. People look at the outward appearance, but the Lord looks at the heart." 1 Samuel 16:7

My neighborhood was rough; it was about two in the morning when I was awakened by the police knocking on the door. I heard my grandfather open the door and talk to police officers, who alleged they were looking for two male suspects that they believed entered our home. Unbeknownst to me and my grandfather, my brother and his friends had been "joyriding" in a stolen car. When they exited the I-94 freeway onto Grand River, they sped by police who eventually chased them into a familiar neighborhood. They ditched the car and began to run. My brother, who knew the neighborhood, came to our home to hide with his friend.

My grandfather let the officers enter our home. I remember them entering my bedroom with a flashlight, not even attempting to turn on the light. They eventually found my brother and his friend hiding in closets. I cannot recall what they were arrested for besides fleeing and eluding the police. This wasn't the first or the last time my brother was arrested. His arrests began slightly after my mother's death when he was sixteen and grieving. I recall him asking my grandparents to move from our crime-infested neighborhood and my grandfather being stuck in his ways, saying he was not leaving the home he had owned since 1952. I witnessed my brother going from being an "A" student in the Junior Reserve Officers Training Corps (JROTC) to selling drugs and stealing cars.

My brother's criminal activities began to take a toll on the family, including myself. One afternoon, I witnessed a neighborhood thug try to attack my grandfather; he was looking for my brother and his friend, who lived across the street. My grandfather tried to stop an assault on our neighbor. When he yelled for the thug to leave, the thug turned around and rushed across the street after my grandfather with a crowbar. My grandfather was so fit that he ran and jumped over our fence and entered the house through the back door. It was hard to sleep after that. I was concerned about the thug retaliating in the form of a drive-by shooting or a subsequent attack on my grandfather.

The summer before ninth grade, I ended up with three staples in my head. I got into an argument with my middle school classmate. He got so mad that he threw a glass bottle at my head when I turned to walk away from him. This same former classmate is currently in prison, serving a 30-year sentence for second-degree murder and for being named the "Drug Kingpin" of Southwest Detroit.

In tenth grade at Cass Technical High School (Cass Tech), I learned that my brother was arrested for a serious offense. He was charged with first-degree, premeditated murder for killing his childhood friend. Allegedly, his friend was found dead in his vehicle. My brother and another person were the last people seen with him on the evening of his death.

My grandfather did not want my brother to go to prison and serve a life sentence, so he hired an attorney, which cost $10,000.00. That was a lot of money back then and still is today. My grandfather had planned to spend his savings on his retirement, but instead, he had to prevent my brother from going to prison. I remember the attorney showing up at our home in a black fur coat, looking like a fly 1990s R&B singer. He sat at the dining room table with my grandfather and other family members, discussing the charges and the legal proceedings.

It was hard to focus on school back then; I just wanted to see my brother. I remember showing up for the last day of the trial when he was scheduled to testify, and the jury was going to issue a verdict after the attorneys made closing arguments. The trial was held at Frank Murphy Hall of Justice in Detroit, Michigan. My brother was very articulate and knew how to use proper English instead of Ebonics (African American English). We always had multiple personas to fit into the neighborhood, at home, and in public around white people. My brother was found not guilty, and I was so relieved.

Nobody at Cass Tech knew what was happening in my personal life; it was hard. I was having nightmares about never seeing my brother again if he got life in prison. I had already lost my mother and grandmother, who died when I was seven and nine years old; I didn't want to lose another family member. I looked up to my brother and wanted to be like him before he started getting into trouble; he wanted to be an attorney. I thought he was so cool between the ages of 16 and 17 because he was the neighborhood barber, DJ, and mechanic and built custom car radio speakers. He also rocked the latest fashion, had a rap album, and introduced the neighborhood to the newest music.

After my brother's trial, I wanted to become an attorney. I told myself if I were an attorney, my grandfather would not have to pay thousands of dollars to prevent our family members from going to jail. It eventually became a theme; my siblings and cousins started getting arrested, and my grandfather was there to bail them out. My twin sister and I are the only two grandkids on my mother's side who have not been arrested.

I dreamt of going to Howard University in Washington, D.C., but I could not afford the tuition, and my standardized test scores were not that good. I also dreamt of being a litigator and attending Howard University like Supreme Court Justice Thurgood Marshall. Although I did not make it to Howard University, I attended college at Grand Valley State University, where I received a full-tuition Business Management Scholarship. After that, I graduated from Michigan State University College of Law (MSU). I did not like law school because I didn't fit in. I felt like most of the white students had advantages because their family members were attorneys and received extra time to take exams due to medical diagnosis. I also had professors who were snobbish and condescending in college and law school, especially when we discussed issues in constitutional law courses that dealt with race. I recall only having one Black law professor, the late Alvin Storrs, whose presence motivated me to attend school every day and do my best.

After graduating from law school, I moved to London, England, for one year. I needed a break to clear my head because my father and my grandfather died while I was in college and law school. When I returned to Michigan, I couldn't find a job at a law firm because my grades were average, so I started my own practice. My mentors were judges like the late Honorable Lucile A. Watts and Honorable Ruthanne Garret, who encouraged me to become an entrepreneur. I met them at MSU alumni events and through family members.

Ironically, my brother became my champion when I started my legal career. He introduced me to his former criminal lawyer, the late Sequoia DuBose, who represented him and my older sister on legal matters. Attorney DuBose allowed me to shadow him. He hired me to draft motions, make court appearances, and even helped me prepare for my first two trials, which I won.

My most memorable trial was before the Honorable Vera Massey Jones. My client was charged with carrying a concealed weapon without a license. It was Deja vu. She was the same judge who presided over my brother's trial and where my first cousin got sentenced to two years in prison for armed robbery. I feared Judge Jones but believed a bench trial would benefit my client. She was hard on criminal defendants carrying concealed weapons, but she knew the law. My client was found not guilty.

The moral of my story is, don't judge a book by its cover. Never assume that successful Black people had it easy growing up. When everything in my life was falling apart, I stayed in school, had a part-time job, and made college-bound friends to prevent me from getting caught up in criminal activity. Cass Tech was my escape route to attend college and get out of my neighborhood. School gave me the tools to become a lawyer and travel the world. I have visited over 10 countries: Egypt, England, Ireland, Scotland, Wales, France, Spain, Kuwait, Belgium, Croatia, Indonesia, Mexico, Cuba, the Caribbean, etc. I also learned that if you keep a clean criminal record, you will have fewer barriers in life, especially when obtaining employment. In some states, employers can legally discriminate against persons with criminal records. I learned this by working in human resources roles and practicing labor law.

Aina N. Watkins, BBA, JD, LLM.

Aina N. Watkins works in the federal sector as a compliance expert on government procurement matters relating to the federal contractor workforce. Ms. Watkins is admitted to the District of Columbia Bar and the State Bar of Michigan.

Aina is a native Detroiter residing in Prince George's County, Maryland. She loves traveling abroad and spending time with her twin sister, Ariane Bigby and her family.

Prior to federal employment, she worked in the private sector practicing Labor & Employment, Criminal, Probate, and Negligence Law.

She has a Bachelor of Business Administration from Grand Valley State University, a Juris Doctor from Michigan State University College of Law, and a Master of Laws in Government Procurement from the George Washington University School of Law.

Aina has published two articles: "Executive Order 13950—On Combating Race and Sex Stereotyping: Its Effect on Government Contractors' Use of Diversity Training", The Procurement Lawyer, ABA Section of Public Contract Law, Vol. 56, No. 4 (2021) and "Direct Threat as an Affirmative Defense in Disability Cases", 15 Digest of EEO Law, No. 3 (2004).

QUESTIONS

1. **Unexpected Encounters with the Law:** Aina's life took an unexpected turn when the police arrived at their home in the early hours, searching for her brother. Reflect on a time when an unexpected event significantly impacted your life or your family's life. How did it alter your perspective or path, and what long-term effects did it have on your aspirations or views?

2. **Family Challenges and Personal Growth:** Aina witnessed her brother's transformation from an "A" student to engaging in criminal activities, profoundly affecting their family dynamics. Think about a time when your family faced challenges or someone close to you changed significantly. How did you adapt to these changes, and what did you learn about resilience and support?

3. **From Trauma to Ambition:** The challenges Aina faced, including violence in their neighborhood and personal injuries, fueled her ambition to become an attorney. Discuss a moment of adversity in your life that motivated you to pursue a specific career or goal. How did this experience shape your future aspirations?

4. **Navigating Academic and Career Pathways Amidst Adversity:** Despite the turmoil in her personal life, Aina achieved academic success and pursued a career in law, inspired by her desire to help her family. Reflect on a time when personal struggles influenced your educational or career decisions. How did you navigate these obstacles, and what impact did they have on your choices?

5. **The Role of Mentorship and Community Support:** Aina found guidance and support from mentors like Judges Watts and Garret, which helped her launch her legal career. Think about the mentors or community support you've had in your life. How have these relationships helped you overcome challenges or pursue your goals?

6. **Reflection on Identity and Aspirations:** Aina's journey from witnessing her brother's legal battles to becoming a successful attorney and entrepreneur highlights a transformative path of resilience and determination. Consider your own identity and aspirations. How have your experiences, especially those involving family and community, influenced who you are and what you want to achieve?

7. **The Impact of Education and Travel on Personal Development:** Aina's story emphasizes the importance of education and the opportunities it creates for personal growth and global understanding. Reflect on how your educational experiences or opportunities to travel have contributed to your personal development. What insights or perspectives have you gained?

8. **Identity and Cultural Heritage in Personal Growth:** Aina's identity and cultural heritage played a significant role in shaping her worldview and ambitions. Consider how your own identity or cultural heritage has influenced your personal growth and aspirations. What aspects of your identity are you most proud of, and how do they guide your goals?

9. **Learning from Failure and Setbacks:** Aina's journey included learning from setbacks and failures, particularly in her early legal career. Share a moment of failure or setback in your life. How did it contribute to your growth, and what lessons did you learn?

10. **The Role of Personal Experiences in Shaping Advocacy and Empathy:** Aina's personal experiences deeply influenced her advocacy and approach to law. Think about how your personal experiences have shaped your views on advocacy, empathy, and justice. How do you hope to use these views to make a difference in your community or field?

Ariane Bigby, Marketing Manager, BBA,MBA,CEBS

"Your beginning will seem humble, so prosperous will your future be." Job 8:7

My name is Ariane Bigby, and I am a product of a Detroit Public School (DPS) education, which has led me to work successfully in the financial service industry for over 20 years. The financial services industry can be defined as banking, investing, and insurance services. This essay reminds me of a disclosure statement in the financial services industry literature: "Past performance is no guarantee of future results." The U.S. Securities and Exchange Commission requires investment firms to add this statement to marketing materials. The statement is added because all investments carry risk, meaning that you could potentially lose all the money that you invest. It's like gambling at a casino; you can win or lose. This statement characterizes my life because your past doesn't dictate your future results. I came from "humble beginnings," but I didn't allow the lack of resources, hardships, and self-doubt to ruin my future. I took risks and invested in myself through education. That may sound corny, but it's the truth.

I grew up on "The Number Streets" on the Westside between West Warren and Grand River during the late 80s and 90s. Detroit was named the murder capital of the world for a few years during this era. My block went from a community of homeowners who cared about their property to one with three crack houses. Besides drugs, there was gun violence, assault, arson, prostitution and theft. The crackheads would even steal my clothes off the clotheslines in the backyard, and the drug dealers would apologize and pay us to replace the items.

My grandfather was the first Black homeowner on the block when he purchased our home in 1952. My grandparents raised me after my mother suffered a mental health breakdown. She became pregnant in college and was forced to come home and get married. In the 1970s, that's just how it was done. My father was physically and mentally abusive, something he inherited from his father. When my parents split, my mom didn't even know she was pregnant with twins. After the birth of me and my twin sister, my mother had a mental breakdown, most likely from postpartum depression. She was a single mom taking care of a set of twins, a 10-month-old daughter and a 7-year-old son. I learned that being a single parent is hard work because having a baby with someone will not make them stick around, and domestic violence should never be tolerated.

My siblings and I were removed from our home and placed with our maternal grandparents. My grandfather was a machinist, a former marine who fought in WWII, and an entrepreneur. My grandma was a housewife who had raised four kids of her own. She helped me with my homework, and we even baked cookies together. My mother visited weekly and brought us toys and books. The books gave me the zest to learn and explore. But tragedy didn't stay away. As she was getting her life together and taking classes at Wayne State University, she died unexpectedly right before my eyes. On Saturday, April 25, 1987, we were expecting a visit, watching the show American Bandstand.

My oldest sister was watching for my mom out of our picture window and saw her collapse near the playground across the street. My grandmother rushed to help her inside the house. I remember my mom sweating and saying she was cold and had to go to the bathroom and saying, "I can see the light." My grandmother screamed and called 911 for an ambulance that never showed up. After an eternity, a police car arrived. The officers carried my mom out of the house in my brother's navy blue sleeping bag. She died from a seizure at the age of 35. Unfortunately, I would learn later in life from my dad that he got my mom pregnant on purpose because all his buddies were getting married and having kids–he was selfish. Young ladies, please take my advice: don't trust these boys when it comes to your bodies. Protect yourself by using a condom or abstaining from sex for as long as you can. Bad choices can deter your future opportunities, just as in the above example.

The following year, in 1988, my maternal grandmother, Bernice, died. She was diagnosed with cancer. It was very painful to see this vibrant, sassy, smart, caring person who was "my mom" battling chemotherapy. It was devastating, but my grandfather, who had recently retired, became a full-time dad with the help of my aunts. He was pretty strict. We were not allowed to hang out with certain people, we had to be in the house before the streetlights came on, and we had to do well in school. We were fortunate to have a village to raise us. I am forever grateful for the structure my grandparents provided, which laid the foundation for my success. I became very self-sufficient. At nine years old, I had to get myself ready for school, do homework, iron clothing, and do laundry.

I attended Harms Elementary School (Harms) for 1st and 2nd grade in Southwest Detroit. Harms had a very diverse population of students. There were Black, white, Mexican and Middle Eastern students. The first time I became conscious of my race was at Harms when a white boy called me a nigger. I recall telling my grandma, and she had to explain what the word meant. My best friend Judy was Mexican and taught me a few Spanish curse words. We loved listening to music; our favorite group then was the Jets. My grandmother decided to take us out of public school for a few years. I believe it was because the environment was changing for the worse. I attended St. Leo's Catholic school from 3rd to 6th grade and returned to the Detroit Public Schools for 7th to 12th grade.

My return back to DPS was at Pelham Magnet Middle School (Pelham). My aunt Denise told us that Olympic gold medalist and track and field star Wilma Rudolph taught at Pelham. I had a great educational experience at Pelham, which prepared me for Cass Technical High School (Cass). My favorite teacher at Pelham was my social studies teacher, Mr. Douguss. He made us read aloud and introduced me to the concept of debate. Pelham was a special "Detroit Compact School," meaning a special school that partnered with over 100 businesses, community organizations and government agencies to assist students with achieving job and college readiness. I remember going to the Whitney restaurant in midtown for lunch, where we were given etiquette training. We learned how to sit at a dinner table and use utensils properly. The training was so awesome. I also ate an anchovy for the first time, which was salty and gross. Detroit Compact also helped me get a job at Detroit Receiving Hospital; I was probably only 12 years old. I answered the telephone for the Patient Guest Relations Department. It was cool and a lot of responsibility. Although Pelham had a great educational program, the social environment took some getting used to.

I met new friends, but I felt like an outsider. My twin sister and I were called names like "white girls." I don't know why, maybe because we dressed differently or used better grammar. I watched TV shows like 90210 and had a subscription to Seventeen magazine, which was probably not typical for a little Black girl in my neighborhood. I also listened to rap and hip-hop music and watched popular Black TV shows. I wore the latest hip-hop fashions but would get style ideas from Seventeen magazine, like wearing Converse Chuck Taylors and flannel shirts like Snoop Doggy Dog when they were not popular with most kids. I was materialistic, so I also had a couple of pairs of Air Jordans. However, I learned that it is okay to be different; it builds character.

The social environment was mayhem. The Detroit Police Department's Gang Squad was present at Pelham frequently. There were fighting and turf wars between the boys from the "Number Streets" and the "Project Kids" from the Jeffries projects. In addition, there were days when my twin sister and I would have to plan our routes walking home from school to avoid being sexually assaulted by the boys in our neighborhood. We would try to stay on the main streets for as long as possible. To feel safe, we would literally have to run home sometimes to avoid wrestling in vacant lots with them. Unfortunately, a few of those boys are dead or in jail for the rest of their lives for murder.

Two girls attended our 8th-grade graduation pregnant. It was heartbreaking to see them becoming single mothers at the tender age of 13. I learned from my girlfriends who lived in single-parent households with lots of siblings that being the product of a teenage pregnancy wasn't good. They were always stuck home babysitting and hated it! I even had a friend who would come to my house and take naps because she could not get enough sleep at home.

I wasn't a perfect kid. I got good grades, but I didn't always follow the rules. I would get into trouble for talking in class. I got suspended from school for insubordination once and was exposed to alcohol and drugs when I was still in middle school. I learned that following the crowd wasn't always the best choice, so I decided being a little different was perfectly fine. Being a good student with good grades allowed me to go to Cass Tech and change my environment.

I am grateful that I had the opportunity to transition to Cass, where I could associate with more like-minded peers and everyone was expected to go to college. There were no gang fights. I felt safe. However, I was sad for the first few weeks because I wanted to attend my neighborhood high school with my friends. My aunts were totally against that, telling me I had to stay at Cass for at least one year; it was the right decision. I met new friends, some still my friends after 25+ years. I learned a lot at Cass. My most memorable teacher was Mrs. McCampbell. She was a tough teacher but exposed me to great literature like the autobiography of Malcolm X. Her class was so enlightening; she made her students proud to be Black and gifted.

My grandfather gave me two options leading up to graduation from Cass: 1) go to college or 2) get a full-time job. He said, "If you don't choose one of those options, you gotta get the HELL out of my house." He didn't believe in taking care of unproductive, lazy adults. I chose to go to college. Cass prepared me academically for college. During the college application process, I realized for the first time that we were poor because the financial aid application required the disclosure of our income. I didn't know I was poor because my grandfather was a homeowner, and we always had basic necessities like water, utilities and food. We even ran errands to the bank with my grandfather and learned how to fill out money orders to pay bills. He responsibly paid the bills first and then set a little aside for savings. Those lessons have stuck with me to this day.

My grandfather taught me to be responsible. I established a good work ethic very early in life. As I mentioned, while at Pelham, I obtained a summer job through Detroit Compact. After that, I received a summer job through the City of Detroit. When I became eligible to receive my food handler's card and work permit, I worked at Burger King and McDonald's while in high school. If I wanted expensive clothing and shoes, I had to buy them myself. Being an excellent student at Cass allowed me to become a Research & Development student at General Motors (GM). I was also given course credits for working at GM.

After graduation, I attended Grand Valley State University (GVSU), where I earned a Bachelor of Business Administration in Marketing. I earned a Master of Business Administration from Wayne State University. Unfortunately, my grandfather died during my junior year at GVSU. He was unable to see my twin sister and I graduate from college. He would have been proud of us because we were the first college graduates in our family.

In life, there are risks. Even with my humble beginnings, I took risks to make it out of my neighborhood by getting good grades in school and staying away from all the illegal activity. I learned that education can take you places and open doors to many opportunities. Please take the time to read, study hard, and strive for a 3.0 GPA or better. To get comfortable with the test questions, begin taking college entrance exam practice tests for the SAT and ACT in the 8th grade. Remember, a four-year college degree may not be for everybody. Getting an associate's degree, enrolling in a skill trades program, enlisting in the military, getting a cosmetology license, or getting another type of certification are all still good options. The key is to have marketable skills to keep you gainfully employed or self-employed. Because you may be less fortunate than others, don't limit yourself by thinking college is out of reach.

In the United States, low-income families are eligible for free training programs, federal grants to pay for school or federally subsidized loans. In addition, Michigan offers a Tuition Incentive Program to eligible Medicaid recipients, and the Detroit Promise program offers free college tuition for qualifying Detroit residents. Dream big, and do not let your environment limit your opportunities for success. Always remember this phrase: "Your past does not dictate your future."

Ariane Bigby, Marketing Manager, BBA, MBA, CEBS

Ariane Bigby is a distinguished professional with over two decades of experience in the financial services industry, encompassing banking, investing, and insurance. A proud product of Detroit Public Schools, her journey from humble beginnings on Detroit's west side to financial expertise is a narrative of resilience, education, and self-empowerment. Despite the adversities faced during her upbringing, Ariane has not only succeeded but thrived in her field, attributing her success to the valuable lessons learned from her past. She holds degrees from Grand Valley State University and Wayne State University, which laid the foundation for her prosperous career. Ariane's story is a powerful testament to the belief that one's future is not dictated by their past, but rather shaped by the choices and investments made in oneself. Her professional journey is marked by a commitment to excellence, continuous learning, and the empowerment of others to achieve their financial goals.

QUESTIONS

1. **Navigating Uncertainty with Optimism:** Ariane's essay highlights her optimistic approach despite uncertainties. Can you recall a time when you faced uncertainty and maintained a positive outlook? How did this optimism help you navigate the situation, and what did you learn about your ability to adapt?

2. **Cultural Exchange as a Learning Tool:** Ariane's experiences underscore the value of cultural exchange for personal growth. Share an instance when engaging with a different culture led to a significant learning moment for you. What was the situation, and how did it enhance your understanding of either the other culture or your own?

3. **Building Resilience Through New Challenges:** In her narrative, Ariane discusses building resilience by embracing new challenges. Reflect on a moment when a new challenge significantly contributed to your personal resilience. What was the challenge, and how did overcoming it strengthen your resilience?

4. **Adapting to Change Through Self-Reflection:** Ariane's journey is marked by her adaptability, facilitated by self-reflection. Describe a period in your life when self-reflection played a critical role in adapting to a significant change. What insights did you gain, and how did they assist in your adaptation process?

5. **Empathy and Understanding in Diverse Environments:** Ariane's story illustrates how empathy and understanding are crucial in diverse settings. Recall a time when empathy helped you connect with someone from a different background. What was the situation, and how did empathy improve your relationship or understanding?

6. **Overcoming Language Barriers to Foster Connection:** Language barriers were a part of Ariane's experience but didn't impede her connections with others. Share an experience where overcoming a language barrier helped foster a meaningful connection. How did you navigate the communication challenge, and what did this experience teach you about connecting across languages?

7. **Family Challenges and Personal Growth:** Ariane witnessed her family's struggles, including domestic violence and the loss of her mother at a young age. Think about a time when your family faced challenges or someone close to you changed significantly. How did you adapt to these changes, and what did you learn about resilience and support?

8. **From Trauma to Ambition:** Ariane's challenging experiences, such as growing up in a neighborhood with high crime rates and personal family struggles, fueled her ambition to succeed in the financial services industry. Discuss a moment of adversity in your life that motivated you to pursue a specific career or goal. How did this experience shape your future aspirations?

9. **Navigating Academic and Career Pathways Amidst Adversity:** Despite the turmoil in her personal life, Ariane achieved academic success and built a career in the financial services industry. Reflect on a time when personal struggles influenced your educational or career decisions. How did you navigate these obstacles, and what impact did they have on your choices?

10. **The Role of Mentorship and Community Support:** Ariane's journey was influenced by the support and guidance of her grandparents and other positive role models. Think about the mentors or community support you've had in your life. How have these relationships helped you overcome challenges or pursue your goals?

Kerrie Trahan

For God has not given us a spirit of fear,
but of power and of love and of a sound
mind." 2 Timothy 1:7

In 2006, after losing my father, scoring poorly on the law school admission test (LSAT), and not being accepted into my dream law school at Cornell University in Ithaca, New York and other preferred universities, I moved from Detroit to Yeosu, Jeollanam Do, South Korea. With this move, I traded the gunshots, defeat, and death surrounding me for South Korea's cherry blossoms, smiling faces and delicious kimchi. I taught English to dozens of elementary and middle school children for sixteen months. Moving abroad would not have been possible without an education and may not have been bearable without my experiences in the Detroit Public Schools Community District (DPSCD).

As a student of the Detroit public school system, I never would have imagined that someday I would travel the world. When I first attended public school, I hated it! I figured transferring from private to public school was a major downgrade. My parents could no longer afford the private school near my grandmother's house in a run-down working-class neighborhood, so I transferred to a public school near my father's house. This was a major adjustment. I was teased for knowing how to read well and called "white girl." I was also teased for wearing a uniform in my new educational environment. Some of my classmates were my neighbors and lived in the surrounding neighborhood known as the University District. Most of those kids were better off than my family and occasionally called me ghetto. Meanwhile, the kids who lived outside the area, those in my grandmother's neighborhood who also attended the same public school, called me "bougie." It was a very confusing time, and I remember feeling insecure and intimidated for the first time in my life.

I grew up quickly in fifth grade and thought I knew who I wanted to be. I believed I needed to be tougher and less friendly. Many of my peers were living in conditions quite different than mine. I remember learning that some students lived with a grandparent or a foster parent or had a parent in jail. On my first day of school in 1995, a classmate (who is now dead) was writing gang signs on the chalkboard while many of the other kids laughed. I felt afraid but, at the same time, excited. This is my first conscious memory of being enthused by "thug life." This was at the height of Tupac's career. I began to think thugs, drug dealers, and even smoking weed were super cool! These people and activities seemed to be admired at school and in my grandmother's neighborhood. I felt my parents were old and committed to raising me in an "old school" fashion. My parents were older than most of my friends' parents, most of whom had them while still in high school or in their early twenties. Everything and everyone I was exposed to at school was new and taboo at home. So, of course, I leaned in. By middle school, I was sneaking to smoke cigarettes with friends at the bus stop and was not as interested in school. I just wanted to be accepted by my peers and someone to "have my back" and be down to fight if needed.

By high school, I had been in fights with fellow students who challenged or insulted me by saying things like, "She thinks she's all that because she's light-skinned with long hair," and all the while, I was fighting myself as self-esteem issues surfaced. By the time I got to the 9th grade, I was more confused and depressed, which led to negative behavior that disappointed my parents. My parents were very hard-working but worked particularly hard at keeping me focused and on track to attend college. Though my father was not a college graduate, he completed a few years of college and understood the value of higher education. My mother has a master's degree, and all her siblings have attended college, many with degrees. Therefore, both of my parents had high expectations relative to higher education. However, many of my friends' parents did not have the same expectations for their children since many did not attend college.

In 10th grade, a friend and I planned to attend a "Cash Money" concert. When I decided to go with another group of friends, she got angry. She spread rumors and told everyone negative things about me. We had the same after-school job at a local dry cleaning service. After a long day at school, I walked into work and heard this girl talking about me to other co-workers. I ran over and punched her in the face! We both got fired and exited the premises with our weave ponytails missing. My father was especially upset, and he and my mother decided that I needed to move in with my father and transfer schools. That's how I ended up transferring to Mumford High School.

Attending Mumford changed my life. My parents were concerned they were losing their grip on me and that my environment was influencing my negative behavior. Upon registration at my new school, my father requested that I regularly meet with a school counselor. The counselor, Dr. Helm, was a petite woman who dressed in African clothing. I remember being impressed by how different and intelligent she was. She lovingly invited me into her office and offered practical solutions to my teenage problems. At first, I was so mad at her! She reminded me that it was against school policy to wear gold chains and leather coats. Mumford is located in an underserved community; students had been robbed (and even robbed each other) for expensive items like these. Still, I wanted to wear my trendy gear and felt completely annoyed by her. After a while, her office became a safe haven for me, and I gladly left my 3-D Versace link chain and leather Davoucci shearling at home.

Right before 11th grade, I moved out of my dad's house, and Dr. Helm reiterated my father's favorite question: "Have you thought about what college you want to attend?" I told her, "No, I need to get this money." She asked, "If I can get you a job at the school this summer, will you do two things: become a Christian debutante, which is a religious service in which the young honorees who are transitioning from childhood to adulthood celebrate their new adult status in the church and attend the Black college tour?" I agreed to do both, not knowing then that they would change the trajectory of my life. While on the Black college tour in Atlanta, Georgia, I called my cousin Kenyatta, who had recently earned a Master's degree from Clark Atlanta University (a historically Black college) and had secured a well-paying job. She picked me up in a drop-top, and we went to Diddy's restaurant and the infamous Lenox shopping mall, where I purchased a pair of Prada sneakers. I won best dressed later that year! I was completely shocked when I realized how cool it was to be a college graduate, self-sufficient and doing well. I started thinking my parents were right the whole time and began to think about my grades seriously. When I returned to Detroit, I went to Dr. Helm's office excitedly. I affirmed that I would move back in with a parent, focus on my grades and begin to look into colleges I wanted to attend.

I graduated from high school in 2002. The day after graduation, I got kicked out of the house again, but I didn't care. I was finally grown and ready to be on my own. Before moving into the dorm at the University of Detroit Mercy (UDM), my mother's alma mater, I lived with friends. College taught me many lessons I had no idea I needed. I sometimes felt it was too expensive, not worth it and even a scam. I often wondered if I would ever need any classes I was paying over $1,000 per class for. Then, there would be moments when I knew I made the right decision, like when I needed to escape Detroit. When my father was killed, I struggled to be in Detroit. Everything reminded me of him. Depression began to resurface, and I even felt suicidal again. I needed a drastic change. I had a friend moving to South Korea to teach English as a second language (ESL) as our contractual job had just ended. When she told me, I said, "Yeah, right." She was serious! She told me I was qualified because I had a college degree. The contractual position we had scoring standardized tests required a college degree. So, I said why not.

Attending Detroit public schools prepared me for living in South Korea because I knew I could navigate unpredictability and unfamiliarity and work with and around people unlike myself. I felt confident and savvy after navigating the streets of Detroit, so I was unafraid to explore the streets of Yeosu, Jellonamdo. While living there, I began to explore the practice of mindfulness. Keep in mind I was still grieving my father's death, and often after work, I would party to numb the pain inside. When my mental health worsened, a friend recommended yoga. At first, I was very stiff and irritated, not knowing what the teacher was saying. The teacher spoke Hangul, and even with the language barrier, I felt relaxed and less anxious after yoga. So, I kept showing up. Eventually, I became hooked on yoga! Yoga made me feel mentally and physically strong in a way I had never experienced. My acne, bad attitude, depression and low self-esteem all subsided as a result of practicing mindfulness (yoga and meditation) regularly. Upon noticing this, I booked trips to meditate in China and detox and practice yoga in Thailand.

Recharged and refreshed, I returned to the States and moved to New York, ready to reapply to law school and achieve my goals. I participated in the Cornell University Prelaw Program. I interned at the New York State Division of Human Rights, where I developed a workplace violence program under NYS Labor Law § 27b. Though this was helpful, I realized that even with the law, morality could not be legislated. Even if a person wanted to violate another person at work, they would, guidelines or not. I started to think critically about how to impact people's hearts, minds and spirits. I thought of yoga and how it had improved my life. I went from being an angry and depressed teen to a grieving and substance-addicted young adult, then to a balanced and healthier young woman and yoga practitioner. This realization led to an epiphany that I could share yoga with people in my city to make our community mentally and physically healthier. My vision was cultivating inner peace to create inner city peace, which gave birth to Yoganic Flow LLC. Our primary mission is to make yoga accessible in the urban community.

Mindfulness changed my life, and I never would have been able to tap into it without an education. Attending Mumford, under the guidance of Dr. Helm, redirected my steps toward college, which was the path my parents had tried to prepare me for. With my college degree, I secured various positions that gave me the experience and tools I needed to build a company. I've worked in Washington D.C. on Capitol Hill as an intern, where I learned how to build a network and speak publicly. I've worked for law firms where I was tasked with compiling contracts and negotiating terms of agreements. I had a chance to work for non-profits, where I gained experience writing grants and cultivating community partnerships. I've had several other jobs that provided me with the skills to grow my company. I took something from every place I worked, and now I teach yoga throughout Detroit to children, adults, seniors, and some of the players of the Detroit Pistons and Detroit Lions.

I knew I wanted to dedicate myself to helping people who faced some of the same things I overcame with mindfulness, like depression, anxiety, suicidal ideation, chronic stress, and pre-hypertension. I faced some difficult challenges in pursuing higher education, graduating and starting my own business. So, every day, I focus on gratitude. The more I focus on what I am thankful for, the more I have to be grateful for. For example, one morning, after writing in my gratitude journal, I received an email from a software marketing company, Mind Body. The company wanted to fly to Detroit to catch footage of Yoganic Flow yoga classes and honor us at their next national conference. At their annual Bold conference, I met Michelle Obama! When I met her, I couldn't help but express my gratitude for everything she did while in the White House and for inspiring me to start gardening again. She was receptive, kind and encouraging and told me my work with Yoganic Flow was needed in our community. Later that year, the First Lady's team contacted me when she visited Detroit. On December 11, 2018, I not only graduated with my master's degree from Wayne State University, but I also opened for Michelle Obama's Becoming book tour at the Little Caesars Arena.

Today, "I am becoming" a leader who has brought yoga to the urban community to empower all Detroiters to take charge of their life in a new way. I am as grateful as ever for having the educational and life experiences that prepared me to contribute to the inner city's health culture and live and walk in my purpose.

Kerrie Trahan

Founder of Yoganic Flow LLC

Kerrie Trahan, a Detroit native and founder of Yoganic Flow LLC, has transformed personal adversity into a mission to bring yoga and mindfulness to urban communities. After facing academic and personal setbacks, including the loss of her father and the disillusionment with her initial law career aspirations, Kerrie's journey led her from Detroit to South Korea, where teaching English and discovering yoga began to heal her grief and depression. Returning to the U.S., she redirected her passion toward fostering inner city peace through yoga, leveraging her education and diverse work experiences to make yoga accessible to all. Kerrie's story is a testament to resilience, the transformative power of mindfulness, and the impact of community-focused entrepreneurship.

QUESTIONS

1. **Cultural Adaptation and Identity:** Kerrie embarked on a significant journey from Detroit to Yeosu, South Korea, in pursuit of new opportunities and experiences. Reflect on a time when you had to adapt to a dramatically different cultural or social environment. How did this experience challenge your identity, and what strategies did you use to navigate these changes?

2. **Educational System Differences:** The essay highlights Kerrie's transition from the educational environment in Detroit to that in South Korea. Think about an instance where you encountered a learning or teaching style vastly different from what you were accustomed to. How did this impact your approach to education or your views on learning?

3. **Overcoming Language Barriers and Miscommunication:** Kerrie's journey involved navigating the challenges of language barriers and cultural misunderstandings. Recall a situation where you faced communication difficulties, whether in a different country or within diverse communities. How did you overcome these barriers, and what lessons did you learn about the importance of communication?

4. **The Role of Mentorship in Personal Growth:** In her narrative, Kerrie mentions the influence of mentors and colleagues in her adaptation and success abroad. Reflect on the role of mentorship in your own life. How has guidance from others shaped your personal or professional development, and what qualities do you value in a mentor?

5. **Resilience in the Face of Adversity:** Throughout her essay, Kerrie demonstrates resilience. Reflect on a challenge you faced where resilience was key to overcoming it. What did this experience teach you about your own strength and capability?

6. **Cultural Misunderstandings and Growth:** Kerrie experienced cultural misunderstandings that led to personal growth. Share a time when a cultural misunderstanding provided you with a deeper insight into another culture or your own. What did you learn from this experience?

7. **The Role of Friendship in Adaptation:** Kerrie's friendships played a crucial role in her adaptation to a new life in South Korea. Reflect on how friendships have helped you navigate a difficult or unfamiliar situation. What have these experiences taught you about the value of friendship?

8. **Perceptions of Home and Belonging:** Kerrie's concept of home evolved through her experiences. Think about your own concept of home and belonging. How has it changed over time, and what factors have influenced this evolution?

9. **Overcoming Stereotypes:** Kerrie confronted and challenged stereotypes in her journey. Recall an instance where you had to confront stereotypes about yourself or others. How did you address these assumptions, and what was the outcome?

10. **Personal Growth Through Travel:** Kerrie's story is a testament to the transformative power of travel. Reflect on a travel experience that significantly impacted your personal growth. What did you discover about yourself, and how has this experience shaped your worldview?

Trina Perryman

"The LORD will guide you always; he will satisfy your needs in a sun-scorched land and will strengthen your frame. You will be like a well-watered garden, like a spring whose waters never fail." Isaiah 58:11

Growing up, I knew what I wanted to be when I grew up a nurse like my Auntie Helen and a dancer/choreographer. But after graduating from Cass Technical High School (CT), fear set in, and I didn't pursue my dreams. I was afraid to leave my family. I didn't know anyone in New York or California where I would have a greater chance of being noticed as a dancer/choreographer. I enrolled at Wayne County Community College District (WCCCD). I changed my major six times in two years. I ended up leaving WCCCD and enrolled at the Computer Learning Center in Madison Heights, MI. I was there for a year and a half and had only two classes left before graduating when the school went bankrupt. I was devastated; that really shook me. Then, I decided to work until I figured out what I wanted to do. I started working at a publishing company. The plan was to get into the company and move into the Information Technology Department. However, because I had so many college credits, I enrolled in Oakland Community College to work on my Associate Degree in Liberal Arts instead. After graduating in 2003 with an Associate Degree in Liberal Arts, I got married and had a baby girl named Reece the following year.

Reece has medical conditions. She has a condition called Cerebral Palsy. Cerebral Palsy is a physical disability that affects movement and posture. She is currently in a wheelchair. She also has epilepsy, which causes seizures. A seizure is a sudden uncontrolled electrical disturbance in the brain. Our daily life is a lot different from most people's. She is 99% dependent on someone else to do basic tasks. Everything that we do for ourselves, we have to do for her. So, it's like doing everything twice. I brush my teeth; I brush her teeth. I comb my hair; I comb her hair.

We are also Reece's eyes, legs, ears, and mouth. It's like having a fifteen-year-old infant. Our parents had to determine what we needed when we were babies based on our cries or behavior. If we were squirming, we probably needed a diaper change. If we were sucking our lips, we were probably hungry. We use the same method with Reece. The difference is her cries are LOUD, and she usually adds a scream at the end for dramatic effect.

We look at the world differently. When visiting family or going into stores, we must ask ourselves: Can Reece's wheelchair fit in the house? Are there stairs? Is there somewhere to lay her down to change her? Is it a smoke-free environment? Do they have animals? Are there accessible parking spaces? *WHEW* We have missed many family functions because Reece's needs could not be met. That bothered me in the beginning, but Reece has taught us to enjoy the simple things in life, like the wind blowing on your face or raindrops falling on your head.

When we could not attend family functions, we would go on adventures with Reece. She loves listening to kids play, so we go to the park or the play area in the mall. She also liked the echoes in the mall. There is one thing that I will not ever get used to.......THE STARES. Reece gets stared at ALL THE TIME. Stares from children are expected. They are trying to figure out what is going on. Sometimes, they just want to push the wheelchair. She LOVES that, so if they ask, we let them. We invite children to ask as many questions as they want. We invite adults to ask questions, too, but they usually don't. Humans usually fear what they do not understand. The best way to understand is to ask questions. If you are out and see a child in a wheelchair, say hi and introduce yourself. The child may not be able to respond verbally, but they may smile or laugh. That small action can make that family's day.

While caring for Reece, Reece's father and I started two businesses: a real estate company and an investment company. I took a six-week real estate course to become licensed as a real estate agent. As a real estate agent, I help families buy and sell their homes. I also became commissioned as a notary public after I saw the need at the real estate company. A notary public verifies signatures on legal documents. A couple of years after opening the business, I returned to school. I attended Siena Heights University in the evenings and obtained a Bachelor's degree in Finance. I then realized I enjoyed learning about the stock market, mutual funds, annuities, and how corporations are built. The stock market (mutual funds included) is owning a piece of a corporation like Amazon, Marc Jacobs or Nike. An annuity is like putting money aside while working to use as income when you can no longer work. I also started researching Warren Buffet, one of the richest men in the world. Reading his books and watching his videos gave me a new perspective on how the rich become and stay rich.

In August 2020, I wrote my first book, *Confessions of a Special Needs Mom: Reece & Me.* In the book, published in June 2021, I share my experiences as a parent of a wheelchair-bound, non-verbal young adult. I hope my 40 pages of confessions enlighten others about disabilities. In March 2022, I published a self-help coloring book, *The World through Reece's Eyes: Introduction to the ReeceWorld Bear Initiative.* This coloring book gives you a sneak peek into Reece's life as a special needs child. The purpose of the ReeceWorld Initiative® is to have a universal symbol that creates awareness. The goal is to ensure law enforcement, first responders, and firefighters know there is a special needs person in the home in the event of an emergency. The ReeceWorld Initiative® decal gives the voiceless a voice. The ReeceWorld Initiative® decal should be placed on the front door and windows of the bedroom where the special needs person resides (www.trina-nicole.com). What I like most about being an entrepreneur is I can work from anywhere. All I need is a phone and a computer. This is perfect for my lifestyle. I get to have a career and earn income, and I am also available for Reece if she needs to go to a doctor's appointment or is not feeling well and needs some cuddles.

While attending Cass Technical High School, I picked the Performing Arts curriculum because of my love for dance. I took dance classes all four years in high school, and I took dance classes in college as well. Most of my hip-hop dance experience came from watching music videos. I still remember the routines to Michael Jackson's Thriller and Janet Jackson's Rhythm Nation videos. In recent years, I've had many opportunities to pursue my passion for dance and learn various dance styles. I've learned ballroom dancing, Chicago-style step dancing, salsa dancing, bop dancing, chop dancing, walk-style dancing and graystone-style dancing. In my first partner dance competition in the Chicago-style step category, I won second place in the World's Largest Steppin Contest in Chicago, Illinois. That was a major accomplishment. The following year, I won first place in two categories: Chicago-style step and walking at The Champions of the Dance Floor in Detroit, Michigan.

I began teaching Chicago-style step dancing with Smoothtivity Detroit in 2014. Smoothtivity is a dance organization that teaches Chicago Style Steppin and prepares students for Chicago Style Steppin dance competitions. Smoothtivity has chapters in Cleveland, Ohio, Dallas, Texas and Detroit, Michigan. I taught the beginner women's class for about a year and then moved up to teaching the women's intermediate class. I eventually taught men's and women's intermediate Step-style classes. I enjoyed showing the students how to make their feet, and the music work together to tell a story. I also learned African dance, modern dance, ballet dance, burlesque dance, and belly dance. I am part of a dance group called The Oh Laa Laa's. We have performed at several events. We have performed as EnVogue, Beyonce, Janet Jackson, Showtime at the Apollo dancers, and Coyote Ugly dancers at a Western-themed event.

Although I did not go to New York or Los Angeles, I could still fulfill my dream of becoming a dancer. Sometimes, life has a different path for you, which may not be what you want. That path is usually curved with detours and roadblocks, but you must keep going. Stay resilient. Keep your eye on the prize: your dreams. Walk in your dreams. If you want to be a doctor, walk like a doctor, talk like a doctor and think like a doctor. If you want to be an artist, visit art museums, dress like an artist, be around artists and stay in creative spaces. Become it in your mind and let it live in your soul.

In December 2019, I started a non-profit organization called ReeceWorld of Michigan. ReeceWorld of Michigan provides support and relief for families with special needs children. In June 2020, we officially received our 501c3 status. The Pandemic and life have not allowed us to have the events we planned. We had a DoubleGood popcorn fundraiser to raise money for supplies for a special needs classroom in the Pontiac School district. We used the remainder of the funds to donate diapers to a student in a class in the Wyandotte School District. For more information about ReeceWorld of Michigan, please visit www.reeceworldofmichigan.com.

Trina Perryman
Reece's Momma, Author, Certified Life Coach and Lover of Dance

Katrina Perryman is a peaceful, free-spirited, nurturing woman who loves to dance by the water. She currently works as a licensed Life & Health Insurance agent, an International dance instructor, and caring for her daughter with special needs full time. Katrina was born and raised in Detroit and currently resides in the Metro Detroit area. She loves dancing, especially partner dancing (Ballroom, Salsa, etc.). Before working in financial services, she was a licensed Real Estate Professional. She has also published two books that she co-authored with her daughter. Trina holds a Bachelor's degree in Finance from Siena Heights University.

QUESTIONS

1. **Facing Fears and Pursuing Dreams:** Trina shares how fear initially prevented her from pursuing her dreams of becoming a nurse and a dancer/choreographer. Reflect on a time fear held you back from pursuing a dream. How did you overcome that fear, and what advice would you give to someone in a similar situation?

2. **Adapting to Unexpected Life Changes:** After the Computer Learning Center went bankrupt, Trina had to reassess her educational and career path. Discuss a moment when an unexpected event forced you to change your plans. How did you adapt, and what did you learn from the experience?

3. **The Role of Family in Personal Development:** Trina's Auntie Helen inspired her to become a nurse. Think about a family member who has significantly influenced your career aspirations or personal interests. How did their influence shape your path?

4. **Navigating Parenthood and Special Needs:** Caring for Reece has profoundly impacted Trina's life and priorities. Share your thoughts on the challenges and rewards of caring for someone with special needs. How can society better support families like Trina's?

5. **Education and Career Shifts:** Trina changed her major multiple times and pursued different educational paths before finding her passion. Have you experienced similar shifts in your educational or career journey? What motivated those changes, and where did they lead you?

6. **Finding Joy in Simple Things:** Despite the challenges, Trina mentions how Reece taught them to enjoy simple pleasures. Reflect on a time when you found joy in something simple or unexpected. How has this perspective impacted your life?

7. **Overcoming Stigma and Encouraging Inclusion:** Trina addresses the stares Reece receives and encourages open dialogue to foster understanding. Discuss the importance of inclusivity and understanding for those with disabilities. How can we promote a more inclusive society?

8. **Entrepreneurship as a Path to Flexibility:** Starting two businesses allowed Trina to balance her career with caregiving. Consider the role of entrepreneurship in achieving work-life balance. What are the benefits and challenges of this path?

9. **Pursuing Passion Later in Life:** Trina eventually embraced her love for dance and achieved success in dance competitions. Share a passion or interest you've pursued later in life. How did it feel to finally embrace this part of yourself?

10. **The Impact of Non-Profit Work:** Through ReeceWorld of Michigan, Trina supports families with special needs children. Reflect on the impact of non-profit organizations and community support. How can individuals contribute to causes they care about, and what impact can these efforts have?

Kawana Baldwin

"My people are destroyed for the lack of knowledge." Hosea 4:6

Moving from the deep south of Mississippi at just five years old to the inner city of Detroit, Michigan, was a bit of a culture shock. My family moved to Detroit in the early 80s for economic advancement opportunities. We moved quite a few times on Detroit's west side before settling into a home. The frequent moves are why I can legitimately and equally claim "7 mile and Joy Road exit 9."

Of course, moving also meant enrolling in a new school. I remember enrolling in Isaac Newton Elementary School in 5th grade and meeting a girl who is still my absolute best friend. We had so much in common; we were quiet, shy and had very old-school parents. We were so close that she was the first and only friend's house I could spend the night over. We used to sing, dance and have fun even though I didn't really know how to dance. But she had all the killer moves. To this day, I'm certain she does not know how much I wished I could bust a move and dance like she could.

In fact, in my pre-teen and teenage years, I didn't believe I had any natural skills, gifts or talents despite coming from a family full of talented individuals. My brother played football, was a natural comedian, could dance and had the gift of gab. My sister played basketball, was and still is naturally beautiful, and is a talented singer, rapper and dancer. My siblings clearly learned all their dance moves from my mother. I recall my mother trying to teach me how to dance, and although I tried, I just couldn't follow the rhythm and flow of the beat. It would impress me how fast my siblings would catch on to new songs and memorize the lyrics. For some reason, I did not catch on to learning music like they did. I can recall the very first song I ever learned, and the only reason I learned it verbatim was because of the method I used to memorize it. That song was "It Takes Two" by MC Rob Base and DJ E-Z Rock. I would play it on my tape recorder and hit stop, play, pause, rewind, play and repeat until I wrote down every lyric. I practiced rapping and singing those lyrics until I knew every word. I still get excited when I hear that song playing on the radio.

Although I could not dance as well as my best friend or siblings, nor pick up the dance lessons my mom was trying to teach me. At 12 years old, I learned the "technique" of styling natural hair and installing hair extensions. I learned from my crafty and creative mother, whose only motivation was to teach me so I could assist with doing her hair. Even though I was never really interested in styling hair, I mastered a "technique" that women were willing to pay for. Another skill I acquired at an early age growing up in the city of Detroit was a fundamental skill most inner-city kids are faced with learning: self-defense. In 6th grade, I was confronted by a girl from my class who was a bully. Without my knowing why, she told everyone she wanted to fight me. Of course, I didn't want to fight her, and I knew she had a big brother who attended our school, too. So, one summer day after school on the playground, everyone gathered in a circle around us, yelling, "Fight, fight." She came toward me, I swung, and the rest is history. Her brother carried her away. She never tried to fight me or bully anyone else again.

At the end of 6th grade, I was devasted to learn my family was moving again, and I was leaving my best friend. We cried like babies, but our parents made sure we stayed in contact. This time, my family moved to the far southwest side of Detroit off Joy Road, where my social skills did not necessarily get any better. Once again, I enrolled in a new school and began my 7th-grade year at Lessenger Middle School. Initially, I had no friends at this school. I was quiet and kept to myself, yet one of my classmates would viciously stare at me, probably because I would ignore her attempt to befriend me. I was reserved, and it generally took me a while to adjust and warm up to new people.

After only a couple weeks of being the new kid on the block, she attacked me out of nowhere outside just after school ended. Of course, I had no choice but to defend myself and fight back. But this time, I suffered an ugly scar on my face after she clamped her fangs into the right side of my jaw. My mother was livid. We found out where the girl lived and visited her house. After a decent conversation with the girl's mother, we learned she was a foster child. Her foster mother empathized with me and acknowledged the girl was a troubled youth. A short time later, the girl left the school. I met some cool new friends later in my 7th and 8th grade years, and we all went to the same high school, Frank Cody High. I cannot lie; I was afraid of attending Cody High School because of the stories my older cousin would tell me about the lady gangs. However, I had no choice since I was not accepted to Cass Tech or Renaissance High School, and Cody was my neighborhood high school.

By this time, I was hustling, braiding and styling hair. I went from just doing my mom's hair to styling and braiding other women's and girls' hair in my parent's basement. My boyfriend at the time (who is now my husband) asked if I was planning to enroll in beauty school after high school. My immediate response was, "No!" I hated standing all day, and my fingers would get numb after braiding for long periods of time. Besides, my true career aspirations were to become a law enforcement officer after being inspired by a police officer who came to speak to my 5th-grade class about the Drug Abuse Resistance Education Program (D.A.R.E.), which was implemented to keep kids off drugs. Frankly, I goofed off my first year and a half in high school, got entangled with the wrong group of friends, and got into another fight that almost got me expelled, but God! I don't know if my faith in God, my grades, or the favor of my praying mother and Godparents kept me from being expelled when everyone else involved got expelled except me.

I remember my Godparents picking me up every weekend. I would stay with them and attend church every Sunday morning. I could only imagine the path I could have easily taken if not for my positive support network and faith in God that kept me covered and placed me back on track. My mother and father were extremely hardworking people who did everything possible to provide the best for my siblings and me. They expected us to attend school every day, get good grades, graduate from high school and attend college. By 11th grade, I began to disassociate myself from certain peers. It was imperative to my future that I started focusing on my post-graduation plans.

Upon graduating from high school, I did not pursue beauty school; instead, I enrolled at Central Michigan University and earned a Bachelor of Science degree in Sociology with a concentration in Criminal Justice and a minor in Psychology. Upon graduating from college, I worked with a non-profit agency in community mental health as a case manager. After three years of working in community mental health, I pursued my career goals in criminal justice and became a parole/ probation agent with the State of Michigan Department of Corrections.

Several years into my career, I was promoted to Lead Agent and later advanced to Workforce Development Specialist. For over 16 years, I helped citizens returning from incarceration restore their lives from criminal destruction to a career-focused path of success as they reintegrated into our communities and restored relationships through Restorative Justice practices. Serving and positively impacting the lives of others gives me great satisfaction, as it has always been my passion.

A decade into my career, I ran into a friend who shared an opportunity with me to earn extra income by selling lash mascara. This encounter reignited my interest in the beauty industry, and God revealed to me that I did not just learn a "technique" from my mother at 12 years old. I acquired a skill from her, and an artistic gift from Him already existed inside me. I was in tears because I never thought I had a natural talent. I never considered styling hair a natural skill or gift; I just thought of it as work.

No, I did not have the same gifts and talents as my sister, brother or best friend. But it was a unique gift carefully wrapped in the hands of God, prepared and hidden in my heart, waiting for me to discover, receive and embrace it. At that moment, I sought beauty school to advance my hair artistry skills and take them to the next level, but not hair in the traditional sense. I yearned to learn and master the art of extending the natural hairs of women's eyelashes. Therefore, on July 9, 2021, with the support of my husband and daughter, I stepped out on faith and resigned from my 16-and-a-half-year career with the State of Michigan to continue my spiritual journey, walking in true passion and purpose.

Today, I am professionally known as the Owner and CEO of The Eyelash Kween, LLC, a Licensed Esthetician, a Master Lash Artist, a Permanent Makeup Artist, and a Licensed Instructor who provides clients with top-notch service, products and educational training. I started this business to help meet the needs of artists locally and globally, focusing on spiritually uplifting, inspiring, and empowering women and helping potential lash artists build their own lash businesses. In all honesty, I can admit it was my social and educational experiences growing up in the inner-city of Detroit and attending Detroit Public Schools that helped shape me into being relatable and empathetic to my client's needs as a professional businesswoman. Education truly is the key to success.

Kawana Baldwin

Owner of The Eyelash Kween LLC

http://www.eyelashkween.com

Kawana Baldwin's journey started in the neighborhoods of Detroit's west side, where she received her education through the Detroit Public Schools system. She furthered her studies at Central Michigan University, where she achieved a Bachelor of Science degree in Sociology focusing on Criminal Justice. Her professional career commenced as a Social Worker in Community Mental Health. From there, she ventured into the Michigan Department of Corrections, where she served as a Parole/Probation Agent. Her dedication and expertise led her to the position of Lead Agent, and she later climbed the ranks to become a Workforce Development Specialist.

Kawana has since become a full-time entrepreneur, proudly owning and operating "The Beauty Bar by Eyelash Kween" in Dearborn Heights, Michigan. She is a multi-talented professional, holding licenses as an Esthetician, Instructor, Master Lash & Brow Artist, and Professional & Permanent Makeup Artist. Beyond her flourishing career, Kawana takes great pride in her role as a wife and mother.

QUESTIONS

1. **Adapting to New Environments:** Kawana's move from Mississippi to Detroit was a significant change at a young age. Reflect on a time you had to adapt to a new environment or culture. What challenges did you face, and how did you overcome them?

2. **Formative Friendships:** The story of Kawana meeting her lifelong best friend in elementary school highlights the impact of friendships. Share a story about a friendship that has significantly impacted your life. How has this relationship shaped who you are today?

3. **Discovering Hidden Talents:** Kawana initially struggled to see her own talents within her family of talented individuals. Discuss a moment when you discovered a hidden talent or passion of your own. How did this discovery change your self-perception or the course of your life?

4. **Overcoming Bullying and Self-Defense:** Kawana's experiences with bullying and learning self-defense are pivotal moments in her narrative. Share a personal experience with overcoming intimidation or bullying. How did this experience shape your approach to challenges and self-confidence?

5. **The Role of Family and Faith:** Kawana credits her family's work ethic and her faith as foundational to her success. Reflect on how your family background and personal beliefs have influenced your career path or life choices. What values are most important to you?

6. **Educational and Career Aspirations:** Inspired by a D.A.R.E. program, Kawana pursued a career in criminal justice before shifting to the beauty industry. Describe how a specific event or person influenced your educational or career aspirations. How have your aspirations evolved over time?

7. **Making a Positive Impact:** Through her work in community mental health and criminal justice, Kawana has been dedicated to serving and positively impacting others. Discuss how you aim to make a positive impact in your community or chosen field. What drives your passion for service?

8. **Embracing Change and New Opportunities:** Kawana's decision to leave her career and pursue her passion in the beauty industry was a leap of faith. Share a time when you took a significant risk to follow your passion or embrace a new opportunity. What motivated your decision, and what lessons did you learn?

9. **Entrepreneurship and Empowerment:** As the owner of The Eyelash Kween, LLC, Kawana focuses on empowering women and helping others build their businesses. Reflect on an entrepreneurial endeavor or project you've undertaken. How does it reflect your values, and in what ways do you strive to empower others through your work?

10. **The Importance of Education and Relatability:** Kawana attributes her success in part to her educational experiences and her ability to relate to clients' needs. Discuss how your educational background or personal experiences have equipped you to meet the needs of those you serve or work with. How do you use education or empathy to enhance your professional or personal relationships?

Shawna Patterson Stephens Ph.D.

"She is clothed in strength and dignity,
and she laughs without fear of the
future."Proverbs 31:25

I pulled my leggings up over my ankles, knees, and thighs as high as they could reach above my waist. I'd grown accustomed to wearing leggings under pants once I started my undergraduate career. While most women around me seemed concerned with their latest love interest, participating in sorority life, or making the grade, I was obsessed with whether my cotton-blend pants rippled over the dimples in my thighs. I worried the expansion of my hips had grown too vast or that my stomach looked too big. I was very precise about each facet of my life. My walk, for instance, was the perfect ratio of control and perceived effortlessness. Step. Back straight, shoulders square. Step. Align walk and reduce thigh overlap. Step. With each window I pass, I look to ensure I've kept my stomach tight. Does anyone else see that bulge? I ate most of my meals alone but made certain to sit with my friends in the cafeteria so no one would notice. I was struggling with body dysmorphia, although, at the time, I didn't realize there was a name for the way I was feeling. And it turns out I had been wrestling with a mental illness for most of my life.

I'll just wear ¾ length shirts to cover my upper arms. I'm too fat to wear shorts. I'll tell them I'm not in the mood to go to Rouge Park. I could never turn it off, but this internal dialogue was louder and more intense in high school. I always considered my size and how I might appear to others. At times, I would avoid going to the pool out of shame. I would tell people I had no rhythm because it was too difficult to control my body proportions when I danced. I was a body politic all of my own. The feeling which emerged from within me was humiliation. I was a captive in my own skin.

In my final year of high school, most mornings started the same. The sun would signal the start of a brand-new day. I would lie on my bedroom floor, feet hooked under the plastic shelf that hoisted our television in the air. I shared a room with my sister, and as she collected those final precious moments of sleep, I quietly finished my last set of sit-ups. Quietly, as not to wake her, I would stand up, gather my running shoes, and tiptoe down the stairs. It was barely dawn as I stretched in the driveway, tied my hair into a ponytail, and began my jog down the street. I would edge around the corner store and into the neighboring community. Street harassment was commonplace. My jog was less stressful when I remained in neighborhoods built for young families. I trained for a race I would never run. I paced myself for a competition that did not exist.

I rode the Warren and Evergreen buses to get to school every day. Since it took me an hour to get to school, I would lie to myself and blame the length of my commute for my failure to eat breakfast each day. I rarely ate breakfast. Or lunch, for that matter. I chose to overload my class schedule to graduate early. I was enrolled in eight periods of courses, and not one of those time slots involved lunch. No one seemed to notice that I marched through each day without taking a break to eat. I didn't remind them. I'm too busy to eat, I would tell myself. I need to go to class.

As a Black girl growing up in the 90s, I did not have access to mental health and wellness resources within my community. There were stores owned by Black folks throughout Detroit, which emphasized the importance of using a holistic health regimen. I just didn't realize they existed. Discussions of themed mental health were fashioned into jokes among my peers and me. Ain't no Black person 'gone go and kill themselves! We often spun false narratives around suicide, depression, and schizophrenia. Are you crazy?! You aren't hearing voices, are you? Eating disorders and cognitive behaviors didn't even register as mental health issues. When considerations for bulimia, anorexia, purging, or body dysmorphia were made, discussions emerged either in health class or in a poorly produced Lifetime movie. That's a white girl problem. I ain't missing no meals...not on purpose! I pretended to find humor with my friends, laughing at their jokes. I also missed meals on purpose. Framed in either of these ways, on television or in health class, it was challenging for us to conceive mental wellness as an issue impacting Black youth. Quite honestly, the word "mental health" was not used widely or even understood among people within my inner circle.

Step. Short breath, sway your arm. Step. You're swaying too much. Step... Damn, she's getting fat! Walking to my locker, I clutched my books tighter to my chest. I knew they were talking about me. They must have been. I was the only other person in the hallway. Most students were in class, but because of my accelerated schedule, I was between periods and needed to switch out my books. Two boys huddle in the darkness outside the lockers down the corridor on my left. I hurried my step to avoid their gaze. With a swift click, I unlocked the steel locker door and began switching out my books. At the same time, I felt the boys enter the hallway behind me. Naw, she's not fat! C'mon, we gotta go! As they turned and walked in the other direction, I frowned. That night, I skipped dinner.

I'm grateful that we are entering a moment where we have a new sense of awareness of all aspects of wellness. Increasingly, we are acquiring access to terminologies and advanced technologies, both of which provide us with the tools we need to manage our health adequately. The concept of intergenerational trauma (which posits that trauma experienced in the current generation can be both environmental and inherited through our DNA) is also circulating more within the communities that feel it most, where we are better able to couch our understanding of our ancestors' past traumas within the ways these wounds inflict pain in our daily lives.

Over time, I have sought counseling and educated myself on body dysmorphic disorder by proxy. I'm a work in progress and must continue to confront past encounters that lend themselves to feeding my illness. Sometimes, I still have really low moments and must find responsible ways to deal with my episodes. Yet, I no longer rely on clothing to define my feelings. I dress in the strength of the Lord. I'm adorned with the dignity I wouldn't allow myself to experience as a young adult. Most of all, I smile as I continue to cast myself into the future at full throttle, always reflecting on how I have permitted myself to grow into the woman I chose to become.

Shawna Patterson Stephens Ph.D.

Vice President and Chief Diversity Officer Central Michigan University

Dr. Shawna Patterson-Stephens (she, her, hers) is an award-winning scholar-practitioner with 20 years' experience in higher education. Dr. Patterson-Stephens serves as the Vice President for Inclusive Excellence and Belonging in the Office for Institutional Diversity, Equity, and Inclusion at her alma mater, Central Michigan University (CMU). In addition to her commitments at CMU, Dr. Patterson-Stephens teaches for New England College. Shawna's research interests include Black and Latinx issues in higher education, media influences in the postsecondary sector, and critical theory in higher educational contexts. She also experiments with various modes of knowledge dissemination to ensure scholarship remains accessible, evidenced through projects like the podcast, "Scholar Tea". Dr. Patterson-Stephens serves as the PI for the Central Michigan University NSF Aspire Alliance for Inclusion and Diverse STEM Faculty Grant. Shawna is currently a co-PI in a national project examining the experiences of Black doctoral women in higher education (Black Women Doctoral Students). Additionally, she is co-editor of "Advancing Inclusive Excellence in Higher Education" (Information Age Publishing).

Dr. Patterson-Stephens enjoys participating in community outreach. In addition to her responsibilities as a board member for the Dr. Melvin C. Terrell Educational Foundation, Shawna contributes to the research writing bootcamp committee for the Sisters of the Academy. Furthermore, she is a board member of CMU's Black Alumni Chapter, the CMU Research Corporation, and recently concluded 4 years of service on the American College Personnel Association (ACPA) governing board. Dr. Patterson-Stephens is a proud member of NCNW, the NAACP, Alpha Kappa Alpha Sorority, Incorporated, The Links, Incorporated, and Jack and Jill of America, Incorporated.

QUESTIONS

1. **Personal Battles with Perception:** Dr. Patterson-Stephens describes her meticulous attention to her appearance due to body dysmorphia. Reflect on a time when you were overly concerned with how others perceived you. How did you navigate these feelings, and what did you learn about self-acceptance?

2. **The Impact of Mental Health Awareness:** Dr. Patterson-Stephens discusses the lack of mental health resources and awareness in her community growing up. Consider the state of mental health awareness in your own community or during your upbringing. How has the conversation around mental health evolved, and what changes do you still wish to see?

3. **Intergenerational Trauma and Healing:** The essay touches on the concept of intergenerational trauma. Reflect on how historical and familial traumas have impacted your own life or the lives of those around you. How do you approach healing, and what resources have been most helpful?

4. **Navigating High School Challenges:** Dr. Patterson-Stephens shares her experience with feeling scrutinized and misunderstood in high school. Recall a challenging time from your high school years that shaped your perspective or identity. How did you overcome it, and who or what provided support during that time?

5. **The Role of Physical Activity in Coping:** Early morning jogs served as a coping mechanism for Dr. Patterson-Stephens. Discuss a physical activity or routine that helps you manage stress or difficult emotions. How did you discover this outlet, and what impact has it had on your well-being?

6. **Dining Alone vs. Social Eating:** Dr. Patterson-Stephens ate most of her meals alone to hide her eating habits. Reflect on your own experiences with eating alone versus in social settings. How do these different contexts affect your relationship with food and body image?

7. **The Journey to Self-Education:** Dr. Patterson-Stephens educated herself on body dysmorphic disorder over time. Share a moment when you took the initiative to learn more about a personal challenge or interest. What motivated you, and how has this knowledge empowered you?

8. **Finding Strength in Faith:** Dr. Patterson-Stephens mentions dressing "in the strength of the Lord" as part of her healing journey. Discuss the role of faith or spiritual beliefs in your life, especially in times of personal growth or recovery. How do these beliefs support your sense of self?

9. **Social Stigma and Humor:** The essay highlights how mental health issues were often the subject of jokes among peers. Think about a time when humor masked deeper issues in your life or community. How do you balance the use of humor with the need for genuine conversation and support?

10. **Aspirations and Inspirations:** Dr. Patterson-Stephens' career achievements are a testament to her resilience and dedication. Reflect on your own aspirations and the inspirations behind them. How do your experiences shape your goals, and what steps are you taking to realize them?

Colonel Robin M. Adams-Massenburg

*"The will of God will not take you
where the Grace of God will not
protect you." Matthew 10:28*

My mother was my greatest fan, supporter, best friend and beloved patient, even when she didn't want to be. She thought calling me "the warden" would scare me off. Her term of endearment only let me know I was doing everything right. I learned key principles from my mom and Marine Father: Look people in the eye, which is simple but lets people know you're paying attention. Give a firm handshake because it conveys the sincerity of the transaction. Allow the other person to speak because it acknowledges you are a genuine listener, and live up to your word because your word is all you have from one human being to another. These small things convey authenticity.

Even as a child, I always wanted to become a nurse. When I was a little girl, every night, my mom came home in her white uniform from St. Joseph's Mercy Hospital on East Grand Blvd., where she was a dietary cook, and I pretended to be her nurse. I told my Mom to look at an imaginary patient, and I told her, "We removed his gizzard." I didn't realize people don't have gizzards.

However, Becoming a nurse seemed impossible to me at the time because my parents were divorced. My mom was only a cook, and there were several other issues plaguing the Black community. My mother often told me to go to school and get a good education because she wanted me to earn more than $7.50/hour like she had earned all her life. I had six brothers ahead of me. Three of my brothers already worked at either Chrysler or General Motors because working at "the plant" was good money, and given my family history, it was my destiny. Teen unwed pregnancies were at epidemic proportions around Detroit during this time. It seemed like girls were drinking some special water; the next thing you knew, they were pregnant. Gangs and drugs were also major issues in the Black community. The Errol Flynns and Blood Killers (BKs) were popular gangs in Detroit in the late 1970s and early 80s. Crack cocaine was prevalent, and getting kids to "just say no" would take more than just a campaign in Black neighborhoods.

I attended two elementary schools, Ralph J. Bunch and Hazen S. Pingree. I was in the last class that graduated from Pingree before it closed and was torn down. I attended Foch Jr. High School on Fairview next to Southeastern High School. Two of my brothers attended Martin Luther King Jr. Senior High School, and three attended Southeastern High School. I was prepared and pumped to become a Southeastern Jungaleer! Plus, I knew all Southeastern High School cheers, had my pom-poms and purple and white paraphernalia, and was ready! My older brothers had paved the way for me in sports and the Reserve Officers' Training Corps (ROTC) there. King was out of my district, and I didn't want to live with my Aunt to go to King, but my brothers had left a great legacy to follow there as well. After graduating high school, another brother attended the United States Military Academy at West Point. That, too, would've been a great legacy to follow.

I was an "A" student throughout middle school. I walked to school with a Jr. High and High School friend. My high school friend dropped out of school in the 11th grade when she became pregnant. So I found another friend to walk to school with, and we later took an aptitude test together. We thought it was another standardized test to get funding for the school, but we learned it was the test to get into Cass Technical High School (Cass Tech). This test was very important to us both because we really wanted to go there. We both passed the test and earned a seat at the best high school in town. Neither of us knew anything about Cass Tech, but grace carried me from one of the worst middle schools to the best high school in the city.

Cass Tech was a huge school. It had eight floors, with over 5,000 students in the building at one time. We had elevators and four staircases, and the whole seventh floor was the cafeteria. I was amazed at the massive size of the school. I had homework every day. I had to get used to the amount of work I received just to keep up. I kept telling myself it was for the greater good. I lost a few friends because they told me I thought I was better than them. I just wanted more for my life than hanging out on a Detroit street corner, getting high and having a baby. My mother worked too hard, and I wanted to make her proud.

I didn't like Cass at first because it wasn't like my neighborhood. I was only one of three African American students in my class, which was intimidating. I made friends with a few other students, and the intimidation faded. I decided to try out for and play on the varsity softball and volleyball teams. I either had to choose gym or another elective. I chose JROTC. ROTC is college-level. The "J" stands for junior. Making the team made me feel good. I didn't like gym, so I asked my mom to take me out and sign me up for JROTC, which was the best decision I've ever made! I excelled and decided I wanted to join the Army after I graduated from high school. I wouldn't lie on a financial aid form just to get funding to go to college and stay home. My mom didn't have the money to send me to college, and I didn't have the discipline to work and go to school. I would've never forgiven my father if he had given me an application for employment at Chrysler to continue his legacy there. So I asked my Mom if she would allow me to join the Army, and she said yes! I graduated with a 'B' overall grade point average from the Business Administration curriculum at Cass Tech, then off to the Army I went. Private First Class (PFC) Adams reported for duty.

The Army was easy in comparison to how I was raised. My mom's standards were much harder. I had to get all As or show her how I tried to get them, so the Army's standards were relaxed to me. The Army also had something my mom didn't have: money for me to go to college. While in the Army, I went to night school and put money away in a college savings plan. I stuck to my plan to stay on active duty for three years, return home, and attend college. When I returned home, I joined the Army Reserves and National Guard to continue paying for my college education. Initially, I was a Combat Medic 91B stationed in Fort Hood, Texas. I became a Transportation Specialist in the Army Reserves and National Guard as I continued to work toward my goal of becoming a Registered Nurse. I received a commission in the Army Nurse Corps as a Second Lieutenant in 1990 and continued my service. I only had 16 years until retirement, but I stayed 26 years and became one of 154 nurses to become Colonel in the Army Reserves.

My dream job was when I served as a hospital's Chief Nursing Officer and as an Assistant Chief Nursing Officer of a hospital twice. When I transitioned from being enlisted to being an Officer, I never abandoned my responsibilities as a nurse, but I didn't get to choose which days I would be a leader. Leading was now a part of my job. The Army Nurse Corps said I must have a Master's degree. My mom said I had to have one as well. I exceeded their expectations. I have two Master's degrees, one in Business Administration and the other in Clinical Nursing. I set the standard high for myself. I knew a Master's in Business Administration (MBA) would help me in executive leadership positions, and the Clinical Nursing degree would give me the clinical edge. I kept my eyes on the prize and positioned myself to be the best and help the organization.

When I decided to retire, I wanted to continue nursing but in a different capacity. I re-engineered my nursing. I consulted with close colleagues and asked them to review my business plan. I also attended small business classes on "how to launch a small business." I created a six-month plan to launch Robin's Nest Solutions in the summer of 2018. This plan allowed me to unwind from the Army and get used to civilian life.

As CEO of Robin's Nest Solutions, I assist veterans in navigating the Veterans Administration (VA) maze. My nursing philosophy was "to help patients move from sickness to optimum health," including their family, environment and faith. When I embarked on the next phase of my life, I took my old nursing philosophy, business plan and everything I learned to re-establish my new nursing philosophy post-Army. It's successfully gotten Veterans the benefits they desperately need and deserve. I love it because it keeps me connected to the military and keeps me "nursing."

Colonel Robin M. Adams-Massenburg

Colonel Robin Adams-Massengerburg is a distinguished figure in military nursing and veteran support. With a career that spans over two decades in the United States Army Nurse Corps, Colonel Adams-Massengerburg has dedicated her life to serving those in uniform and continued her commitment to care through her innovative work post-retirement.

Graduating with honors from Cass Technical High School, Colonel Adams-Massengerburg joined the Army, initially serving as a Private First Class. Her drive and determination saw her quickly rise through the ranks, receiving a commission as a Second Lieutenant and eventually achieving the esteemed rank of Colonel. Throughout her military tenure, she held various pivotal positions, including Combat Medic, Transportation Specialist, and ultimately, Chief Nursing Officer. Her leadership and expertise were instrumental in advancing the standards of military nursing care and mentorship.

Recognizing the importance of continuous education, Colonel Adams-Massengerburg has two Master's degrees in Business Administration and Clinical Nursing. This academic achievement not only broadened her administrative and clinical capabilities but also positioned her as a leader in nursing and healthcare management within the military and beyond.

Upon retiring from active duty, Colonel Adams-Massengerburg transitioned her focus to addressing the needs of veterans through the founding of Robin's Nest Solutions in 2018. As CEO, she leverages her vast experience and insight to provide invaluable assistance to veterans navigating the Veterans Administration system. Her work through Robin's Nest embodies her nursing philosophy of holistic care, extending support to include not just the veterans but their families, environment, and faith. Her efforts ensure that veterans receive the recognition, care, and benefits they have earned through their service.

QUESTIONS

1. **Resilience and Adaptability:** Colonel Adams-Massenburg faced numerous challenges but adapted and thrived in various environments. How have you shown resilience and adaptability in your life, especially when encountering new or challenging situations?

2. **Career Aspirations vs. Reality:** Initially dreaming of becoming a nurse, Colonel Adams-Massenburg's path led her to the military and then to an entrepreneurial venture. How have your career aspirations evolved over time, and how have you navigated changes in your professional goals?

3. **The Impact of Family and Community:** Her mother's guidance played a significant role in her life. How has your family or community shaped your values and decisions?

4. **Overcoming Societal Challenges:** Colonel Adams-Massenburg overcame societal challenges, including those specific to the Black community. What societal challenges have you faced, and how have you worked to overcome them?

5. **The Role of Education:** Education played a crucial role in Colonel Adams-Massenburg's journey. How has your educational journey influenced your life and career?

6. **Leadership and Service:** Her career in the military and as a nurse exemplifies leadership and service. How do you define leadership, and what does service mean to you?

7. **Transitioning Between Roles:** Colonel Adams-Massenburg transitioned from military to civilian life and entrepreneurship. How have you managed transitions in your life, and what lessons have you learned from these experiences?

8. **Following One's Passion:** Despite the initial deviation from her nursing dream, she eventually found a way to integrate her passion into her career. How have you pursued your passions, and how have they influenced your career choices?

9. **Veteran Affairs and Social Responsibility:** Her work in helping veterans navigate the VA system highlights social responsibility. How do you engage with social causes or community service, and why do you think it's important?

10. **Legacy and Influence:** As a woman who has broken barriers and served as a role model, what legacy do you hope to leave, and how do you wish to influence others?

Detective Melinda Cook

"For I know the plans I have for you," declares the LORD, "plans to prosper you and not to harm you, plans to give you hope and a future. Then you will call on me and come and pray to me, and I will listen to you. You will seek me and find me when you seek me with all your heart. I will be found by you," declares the LORD, "and will bring you back from captivity. I will gather you from all the nations and places where I have banished you," declares the LORD, "and I will bring you back to the place from which I carried you into exile." Jeremiah 29:11-14

There is no glitz and glam to my life. No short story that reads "Mackenzie High School alumnae goes on to Michigan State to graduate with honors". There is no tale of a little girl growing up and marrying a rich doctor with a white picket fence and a dog named Spiky. This journey of life has been eventful for me. I have had some ups, downs, turnarounds and all-arounds. BUT WAIT! Do not count the little Black girl from Detroit out just yet. I am Detroit's Finest. My trials are my victories!

On March 20, 2020, I became a Detroit Police Officer-"Detroit's Finest." Becoming a police officer was not easy, but when Jesus says yes, nobody can say no. Becoming a Detroit Police Officer was one of the best decisions I ever made in life. I am proud of myself for beating the odds. Many said that a person like me could never become a police officer, especially not at the age of 40. Still, the love I have for helping people, my community, working with youth and my family would not let me fall victim to the naysayers. I worked hard to accomplish one of my lifelong dreams and became one of "Detroit's Finest."

Growing up in Detroit wasn't normal. I grew up with eight brothers and parents who were alcoholics and drug addicts. Despite years of substance abuse that plagued my home and upbringing, I believed I would one day beat the odds. I watched some of my brothers fall victim to the streets and be incarcerated, but with a lot of prayer, those siblings turned their lives around and are now living productive lives with beautiful families.

Our youth must have a dream, vision, plan, positive influences, and outlets to become successful so they don't lose sight of their goals and aspirations and let mishaps sneak in. Some of my friends with whom I shared dreams and laughs took on adulthood too early. I witnessed many teens become pregnant or abuse their bodies with illegal substances. As I prayed for myself, I never stopped dreaming and praying for my friends.

My other dreams were to become wealthy and never struggle with poverty again. I wanted a life where fairy tales came true. I also wanted to help my family and others in my community. I believed that if I worked hard, I could do anything I put my mind to. However, no one ever told me as a child the road would become so difficult, thieves would come to steal my youth, and my own mental health would be my biggest opponent.

By age 15, I had seen a lot and endured plenty of pain. My nights were sleepless, and I was starting to lose hope. As a teen, I didn't know what mental unhealthiness was. The effects of my parents' mistakes had caused some unspoken trauma in me. A close relative and a family friend sexually abused me. I had developed so many insecurities that I could not smile. The restrictions of a limited household income kept my siblings and me feeling bound up inside. The only blessings I thought I had were my dreams, goals and my exceptional track running ability.

I journeyed through life, running quickly and attempting to jump any hurdle that came my way. I was searching for the place where fairy tales came true. I no longer wanted to be reminded of my mistakes or my parent's shortcomings. I ran, and I ran. I was running here and there and everywhere in pursuit of happiness.

Then, one day, my running stopped. It was a sunny Saturday in June of 2012. I was traveling to Texas to establish permanent residency, but that day, God spoke to me in a voice I'd never heard before. The voice was so clear and bold. The voice said, "You have run all you can. You have fallen, and I have lifted you only for you to run again. Your dreams were never denied; they were just delayed." Without warning or special goodbyes, I relocated back to Detroit after being gone for 13 years. I cried and struggled with my decision to return home to Detroit. I second-guessed myself about the voice I heard. Could the voice I heard have been my imagination? With my best friend of six years in tow, I didn't have much time to think about things; I just had to do it.

On October 1, 2012, I began to walk in my destiny. I finally slowed my pace down. I began to believe in myself again, find positive outlets and follow the word of God. I worked harder than ever in my community. I did not let the negative portrayals of the "New Detroit" discourage me. I began to minister and work with the youth in the city. I served older people and all those who needed assistance.

I was brought back to Detroit to showcase my Black Girl Magic. If I kept running, I would've never seen my trials become victories. I am one of "Detroit's Finest" and a young Black Girl from Detroit with dreams. God never denied my dreams; they were just delayed. My dreams came to pass according to God's plan. When I set my own road map aside and adjusted myself to God's road map for my life, I began to see my victories.

I obtained a degree in Criminal Justice as God promised. I worked for the United States Government as a background investigator, working directly under the Federal Bureau of Investigation (FBI) for several years. I took advantage of the opportunity to teach K-12 students, coach a championship track and field team, coach middle school volleyball, become a youth director, and start three of my own lucrative businesses. Yes, my dreams were becoming a reality.

The race of life is not about how fast you can get to the finish line; it's about staying the course and finishing the race. My race needed to be slowed down so that I could see the beauty in my city. My journey back to Detroit from Texas helped me to reflect on the good that came from being a DPS (Detroit Public Schools) grad. I also had the opportunity to reflect on those who paved the way for me.

I am the woman I am today because of the great people placed in different segments of my life to help show me the way. I dedicate this short story to my fifth-grade teacher, Mrs. Ayers, for always being a phenomenal role model when no one was looking; my Mackenzie High School track coach, Jane Chapman; my 12th-grade English teacher, Ms. McMillian; my Co-Op teacher, Dr. Richard James and the late Pastor David Ford.

You are destined to be what you are called to be.

Detective Melinda Cook

Born and raised in Detroit amid adversity, Detective Melinda Cook emerged as one of "Detroit's Finest," a testament to her unwavering spirit and faith. Facing a childhood shadowed by her parents' struggles with addiction and navigating personal and societal challenges, Detective Cook never lost sight of her dreams. Her journey is marked by a profound connection to God, guiding her through trials to triumphs. At 40, she defied expectations, becoming a Detroit Police Detective, embodying hope and determination. Detective Cook's life, enriched by her commitment to her community, youth, and family, showcases the transformative power of faith, hard work, and the belief that dreams delayed are not dreams denied.

QUESTIONS

1. **Turning Trials into Victories:** Melinda speaks powerfully about turning her trials into victories. Reflect on a personal challenge that you transformed into a victory. What was the situation, and how did you overcome it to emerge stronger?

2. **The Power of a Support System:** Melinda credits significant figures in her life for their guidance and support. Think of someone who has been a crucial part of your support system. How have they helped shape who you are today, and what specific role did they play in your journey?

3. **Overcoming Barriers with Determination:** Despite facing barriers, Melinda achieved her dream of becoming a Detroit Police Officer. Share a time when you faced significant barriers to achieving a goal. How did you overcome these obstacles, and what drove your determination?

4. **The Role of Faith in Personal Journey:** Melinda's faith played a critical role in her life decisions and resilience. Discuss how faith, spirituality, or a personal belief system has influenced your life decisions and helped you through challenging times.

5. **Rediscovering Self and Purpose:** Melinda's return to Detroit was a pivotal moment in rediscovering her purpose. Describe a time when you had to make a significant decision that led to self-discovery. What was the decision, and how did it help you find or redefine your purpose?

6. **The Importance of Community Engagement:** Melinda's work in her community and with youth is a testament to her commitment to service. Reflect on an experience where you engaged with your community or worked to make a difference in the lives of others. What motivated you, and what impact did it have on you and those you served?

7. **Adapting Dreams to Life's Realities:** Melinda learned that her dreams were not denied, just delayed. Share a personal experience where you had to adapt your dreams to the realities of life. How did you adjust, and what was the outcome?

8. **Mentorship and Passing on Knowledge:** As a teacher and coach, Melinda passed on her knowledge and experience to others. Discuss a time when you mentored someone or passed on your knowledge. What was the context, and how did it feel to contribute to someone else's growth?

9. **Finding Beauty in Your Own City or Community:** Melinda's journey helped her see the beauty in Detroit. Reflect on a moment when you gained a new appreciation for your own city or community. What changed your perspective, and what beauty did you discover?

10. **The Journey Back to Self:** The journey back to Detroit was crucial for Melinda to slow down and appreciate her life's course. Share a journey you've undertaken (physical, emotional, or spiritual) that led you back to a deeper understanding of yourself. What did you learn about yourself, and how did this journey change you?

Joyce Sanders

"God is our refuge and strength, an ever-present help in trouble. Therefore, we will not fear, though the earth give way and the mountains fall into the heart of the sea, though its waters roar and foam and the mountains quake with their surging."
Psalms 46:1-3

Everywhere I go, I run into people from Detroit who attended Detroit Public Schools (DPS). They are successful people who are doing great things in their communities and throughout the country. However, it doesn't matter what school you attend. What matters is your focus and ambition. A determined, focused person can go to the worst school and succeed. You should remember to put in the time and effort to become who you want to be.

I attended DPS for my entire K-12 educational career . During that time, I had teachers that lived on my street. I would see those teachers at school and then come home. They were friends with my parents, so I was always on my best behavior. It's amazing to see many of the teachers who were just starting when I was in high school still teaching and now teaching my children. It is an incredible feeling to know my children are in good hands. My elementary and middle schools were within walking distance from my house, and most of my friends went to the same schools and lived in my neighborhood. The relationships I established with those friends in school have lasted 30-plus years, many of whom I am still friends with today.

In school, I didn't get the best grades, have the best study habits or take advantage of all the opportunities available. This is one thing that I regret most. There was a summer program that I signed up for and did not attend when I got accepted at Michigan State University (MSU). The program was for the business school, which would have prepared me for what was ahead. If I had taken the class, I would have known what to expect when I arrived on campus and could have made some great networking connections. Instead, I was totally lost when I got to MSU.

I had no idea the College of Business was so competitive. In my mind, it was like high school. You go there, you pass classes, and you graduate. The College of Business had criteria for acceptance that I had no idea about, so when I did find out, it was too late for me to improve. The GPA needed to enter the College of Business was 3.0 overall for all business classes. However, because so many students wanted a business degree, I needed a much higher GPA in those classes to be considered. Going home or transferring to another school wasn't an option for me. I wanted to finish school at MSU, where I started, so I changed my major to Merchandise Management because most of the core classes were the same for a business major. This meant I did not have to start over and only had to stay in school for an extra year to graduate. Even though I had setbacks, I was able to graduate and eventually accomplish great things.

I graduated from MSU in May 2002, eight months after the World Trade Center attacks. After graduation, I went on many interviews, and no one seemed to be hiring then. I would have become a retail buyer if I followed that career path. However, I honestly could not see myself working retail hours. I had previously worked in retail and desired a career with a nine-to-five schedule. So, instead of seeking a position in retail management, I chose to go a different route. I moved back home to Detroit and worked a few different jobs before I found the one that was right for me. I worked in a furniture store, in retail banking as a teller, and finally, in collections for a car company. Working in collections at Chrysler Financial helped me build my customer service skills with opportunities for advancement in a field I really liked.

The economic downturn of 2008 caused me to be laid off from the job in collections that I thought showed so much promise. Because of this setback, I decided to take classes at H&R Block to become a tax professional, but I was called back to Chrysler Financial. I decided to work both in collections and as a tax professional. A year later, I applied for a position with the Internal Revenue Service. I got the job and have been employed with the federal government ever since. I've worked in various departments throughout the Federal Government, including the IRS and The Veterans Health Administration.

I'm currently working with the Department of Defense as a Contract Administrator, and this is a position that I absolutely love. I became fully certified in my current position at the end of 2021. This certification allows me to be a Contract Administrator or Specialist anywhere in the world, increase my job responsibilities and access more opportunities for advancement.

Every position I've had in the past prepared me for where I am today. I worked hard and even worked some jobs I absolutely hated, but I stayed to learn what was needed to get me to the next level. Knowing what I have done to get where I am today is most important to me. All the skills I acquired prepared me for this very moment, and I use many of those skills daily.

My current goal is to turn these experiences into entrepreneurship (owning a business). Today's world is much more open to entrepreneurs, and with the internet, it is easier to reach people worldwide. The internet and social media allow you to market your product or service to more people. Now is the perfect time to turn things you enjoy doing into a profitable business. I have two sons, which is one reason I've been so focused on making a better life for my family. I am currently deciding on ways that I can invest, as well as brainstorming ideas for entrepreneurship. I want to have several sources of income, which will help if there's an economic downturn. I want to show my boys that they can succeed in doing things they enjoy and have financial freedom.

I have learned that being patient is one of the most important things in life. Sometimes, I could honestly say that I was ready to walk away from everything I learned, earned, and worked for. There were times when I thought that I would be in a job that I hated for my entire life. Getting up in the morning and going to a job you hate is so difficult. It affects your performance and adds lots of stress to your life. It's much easier to make money doing something you love.

One thing I wish I had done and that I suggest everyone do is, before you choose your career path, sit down and research what it is that you want to do. When I was younger, I always wanted to be a lawyer, but for some reason, that was not something I ever pursued. Many self-help books and how-to manuals are available on choosing your career path or starting your own business and making it profitable.

Providing generational wealth for my children and guiding them to make the best decisions for themselves is what I hope to accomplish. I was once told, "If you do something you love, then you never work a day in your life." It's a quote I have seen for some time, so it wasn't something that someone necessarily told me, but I saw it often. Create a life that has a life-work balance. It's very important to make sure that you enjoy life, not just "go to work," because life is too short, so having fun and enjoying life is very important. Work hard, but play even harder; you will get the best out of life. The years after high school go very fast; soon, you grow up and must go to work every day. My advice to you is if you go to college, enjoy it. Make sure you take time to travel and see the world and go to a place you may have always wanted to go. Do things you enjoy, make time for trips, and spend time with friends and family. Once you become an adult, you do not want to be a person who lives for the weekend. Weekends are fun, allowing you to rest and relax after a stressful work week, but it's best to do something you enjoy.

Remember, you can be anything you want and do anything you want. Make sure you research what you want to do and learn all you can about it. It does not matter where you are from. What matters most is putting your all into anything you do.

Enjoy your life and live it to the fullest.

Joyce Sanders

Joyce Sanders has two extremely important roles in her life. She is a Contract Administrator for the Defense Management Contract Agency (DCMA) in Detroit and she is the mother of two boys. She can often be found at her kids' football and soccer games rooting them on. In her spare time, she is a voracious reader.

QUESTIONS

1. **Influence of Early Education on Success:** Joyce Sanders speaks highly of her education within the Detroit Public Schools system and its impact on her and others' success. Reflect on your own early educational experiences. How have they shaped your ambitions and contributed to your personal and professional success?

2. **The Importance of Seizing Opportunities:** Joyce regrets not attending a summer program before college, which she feels could have better prepared her for university challenges. Recall a time when you missed an opportunity. How did this affect you, and what lesson did you learn about the importance of seizing opportunities when they arise?

3. **Adapting to Unexpected Academic Challenges:** Joyce had to change her major when she realized her initial choice's competitive nature and requirements. Share a moment when you faced an unexpected challenge in your academic or professional life. How did you adapt, and what did this experience teach you about flexibility and resilience?

4. **Navigating Career Path Post-Graduation:** After graduating during a tough job market, Joyce worked in various roles before finding her path. Discuss a time when you had to navigate uncertain or challenging professional waters. How did you find your way, and what did these experiences teach you about perseverance and self-discovery?

5. **Building a Career Amid Economic Uncertainty:** Joyce's career was significantly affected by the 2008 economic downturn, leading her to explore and adapt to new opportunities. Reflect on a time when external factors like the economy influenced your career decisions. How did you manage these challenges, and what strategies helped you overcome them?

6. **The Role of Continuous Learning and Certification in Career Advancement:** Joyce achieved certification that broadened her career opportunities. Discuss the importance of continuous learning and professional development in your life. How have they impacted your career trajectory or personal growth?

7. **Entrepreneurship and Financial Security:** Inspired by Joyce's goal of entrepreneurship for financial independence and generational wealth, think about your aspirations in entrepreneurship or financial planning. What steps are you taking to secure financial freedom and stability for yourself and potentially future generations?

8. **The Power of Patience and Passion in Achieving Career Satisfaction:** Joyce emphasizes patience and the pursuit of a career that brings joy rather than stress. Reflect on how patience, passion, and perseverance have played a role in your career choices. How have these elements influenced your job satisfaction and overall well-being?

9. **The Importance of Research and Planning in Career Selection:** Joyce advises thorough research and planning before choosing a career path. Share how you approached the decision-making process for your career. What resources or strategies did you find most helpful, and how did they influence your final decision?

10. **Life-Work Balance and Enjoying Life:** Joyce highlights the significance of balancing work with personal enjoyment and making the most of life. Discuss your approach to achieving a healthy life-work balance. What activities or practices help you enjoy life while fulfilling your professional responsibilities?

Danielle Smith

"Where there is no guidance, a people falls, but in an abundance of counselors there is safety."
Proverbs 11:14

I can't express enough how much guidance, support, love, and counsel I found on the grounds of Denby High School. Denby was the one place I spent more time than home for four years. I was rarely absent, attended all the sports events, participated in some after-school activities, and even took driver's training during the summer because my friends had to attend summer school. I spent plenty of time with teachers, counselors, administrators, and parent volunteers. My grades were always in order. I did what I was supposed to do for the most part. I had good relationships with the people there. Denby was home to me. Did I love it there? Yes. Did it properly prepare me for what was next – after high school? No. Did it live up to its fancy name at the time, "Denby Technical & Preparatory High School?" Not to me. I can't recall much technical material in the curriculum, and I wasn't prepared for anything to come after high school.

I was a top–honor roll student of the graduating class of 2002. I attended honors classes for four years and received awards for outstanding academics, foreign language, and citizenship. I achieved an overall GPA of 3.5, my SAT scores were amazing, and I had acceptance letters to top colleges in the state. I even scored a few 4.0s during that time as well. I was considered a smart girl. On paper (meaning a transcript), I looked bright, like I was going places when I had no idea what I wanted to do or be after high school. I knew I was expected to go to college and should aim to get a job with a company with good benefits and an opportunity for a career path. I can't say that's how it turned out, but I tried.

As I prepared to take senior pictures in the fall of 2001, I was in a life-changing situation. I was pregnant, scared and confused. I was never the girl to play house. I had a baby brother, but I never changed his diapers or cared to babysit; my big sister did that. It was me, the smart, good girl pregnant at seventeen. I was embarrassed, but not enough to have an abortion. I hid my pregnancy until about four months, but I chose to have my child. I had to move past embarrassment to acceptance. My family was on board. I continued to go to school literally until I gave birth. Other parents and some family judged me, but I was never ridiculed or excluded by any of the administration/staff at Denby. I felt supported and safe there during an uncomfortable time for me. I was encouraged to continue with my college plans and did just that.

I enrolled in Wayne State University, starting in the fall after graduation, and I felt so small on day one. I was running late and very frustrated with the classes being all over campus. I sat in English 101 looking at the syllabus, feeling like there was a gap in the information. I was behind academically compared to other students who progressed smoothly through the curriculum. However, English was my favorite subject; I maintained an A in high school. It appeared that the quality of my high school education was below that of other schools, possibly due to a lack of resources, funding or teacher training. Unlike my Denby days, my time at WSU was short-lived; I dropped out after one semester. It was a challenge for me. I didn't have any family in college. I can't recall how many college trips we had at Denby and why I didn't attend any. I wasn't prepared for the rigorous coursework or the realities of attending a university.

Despite the inadequate education, the moral support and genuine care provided by the school community at Denby was top tier, creating a positive and uplifting environment for me as a student. But honestly, the school failed to provide the necessary academic preparation for me to excel at a university. Ultimately, I graduated with an Associate of Arts degree from Wayne County Community College. I finally had the degree, but never quite got the corporate career. I worked in multiple industries before exiting the workforce. I became a full-time entrepreneur in June 2020 and haven't looked back.

Danielle Smith

Entrepreneurship was not on my radar back in my school days. I don't think I fully understood the word until I lived it. Although my father didn't have a job and my cousin had a nail shop, I was unaware that working for oneself was a viable career option until later in life. Traditional education and employment models were emphasized more heavily in my upbringing and education. When I was in school, there was little to no information about owning and operating a business; I hope this has changed. There were approximately 31.7 million small businesses in the US in 2021. With the percentage of female entrepreneurs in the US steadily increasing, young female and male students must be aware of all options aside from attending a college or university after high school. Students should be more exposed to real-life situations and opportunities where they can explore their own passions as opposed to completing an abundance of equations most will never use again outside of class.

I am a serial entrepreneur. I started as an entrepreneur following my passion for planning and enhancing spaces. I became an event planner and decorator in 2013, but technically, the first event I planned and decorated was in 2002, my baby shower. I didn't know everything when I started, but I started. I was eager to learn and grow my business. I took classes and mentorships and invested in myself with a goal to brand and elevate. For years, I worked a full-time and part-time job and operated my business on the side. In 2020, I took a leave of absence for three months, hyper-focused on my business and saw tremendous growth in sales and revenue during that short time. I made a risky decision to leave my job and focus on my business.

A risk worth taking, in 2021, I opened the doors to First Class Event Suite, my very own event space based in the same city/neighborhood where I grew up. My brothers, father and family, and I created a beautiful, open, and classy 2900 sq. ft. event space in the heart of the hood. Often referred to as "The Suite," the venue has a reputation for class and cleanliness through our first-class customer service and the success of our events. We have held countless events of varying sizes and themes; clients always leave rave reviews and refer their friends and family. We are dedicated to creating unforgettable experiences for our clients and plan to be around for a long time.

In addition to this business, I also operate a property management and investment business with my dad and brother. I am a business credit coach. Lastly, I am a newly licensed real estate agent looking forward to helping many families become homeowners. I would not recommend anyone to do as I did; however, if provided the opportunity, I would do it again. I often say God blessed me when I decided to keep my child at such a young age. My son has never given us any problems; he is an amazing role model for his little brothers. He is dedicated to his goals and works very hard. I am fortunate enough to wake up daily and do what I love. I pursue my passions and provide for my family at the same time. Despite the challenges, I have inspired many to work hard and go after what they want. Somehow, I have become that safe place for others that Denby once was to me. I provide guidance, counsel, and support to many about entrepreneurship, business, motherhood and more.

In conclusion, despite the inadequacies in my education, I am a proud former DPS Student. I admire the teachers, administrators, and staff who get up daily and teach at our public schools. I appreciate those I came across during my time. I know that the problem in the school system goes much further than the walls of my alma mater. Academically, I thrived while I was there. I flourished socially, and my mental health was intact as an inner-city teenager. There was a sense of home, comfort, and safety, which allowed me to be me. Much is to be said about the Detroit Public Schools System, but I can't say it completely failed me.

Danielle Smith

Danielle Smith grew up on the East side of Detroit. She was the second oldest in a blended family of 10. After numerous jobs & graduating college, in 2013 Danielle began to explore entrepreneurship. She found her passion in the events industry, as a successful event planner, decorator & balloon stylist. In 2020 she went full time entrepreneur, opened a venue (First Class Event Suite) in 2021 and has yet to look back.

Danielle is a proud mother of three boys, her oldest is an elite college football player. She is a business and homeowner, who operates and resides in the city. A serial entrepreneur, Danielle is a property manager and licensed realtor.

QUESTIONS

1. **Exploring Career Paths Through Research and Planning:** Danielle's journey underscores the importance of guidance and self-awareness in career selection. Reflect on your own career decision-making process. How did you research and plan your career path, and which resources or strategies were most instrumental in shaping your decision?

2. **Achieving a Healthy Work-Life Balance:** Danielle highlights the significance of balancing professional responsibilities with personal happiness. Describe your approach to maintaining a work-life balance. What specific activities or practices have you found effective in managing this balance while ensuring personal fulfillment?

3. **The Importance of Community Support in Overcoming Personal Challenges:** Reflecting on Danielle's experience during her pregnancy, how has community support (from schools, workplaces, or other groups) played a role in helping you through a personal challenge? What was the nature of the support, and how did it impact your situation?

4. **Preparation for Life Transitions:** Danielle felt unprepared for the academic and social demands of college. Share an experience of a significant life transition you have faced. How did you prepare for it, and looking back, what would you have done differently?

5. **Considering Entrepreneurship as a Viable Career Option:** Based on Danielle's eventual success as an entrepreneur, discuss your views on entrepreneurship. Have you ever considered starting your own business, or do you know someone who has? What do you perceive as the main challenges and benefits of this career path?

6. **The Impact of Early Life Decisions on Future Outcomes:** Danielle's decision to become a mother at a young age significantly influenced her life path. Reflect on a pivotal decision you made at a young age and its long-term impact on your life. How did this decision shape your personal and professional journey?

7. **Finding Success Outside Conventional Career Trajectories:** Despite not following a traditional career path, Danielle found fulfillment and success in entrepreneurship. Discuss your experiences or aspirations regarding non-traditional career paths. How do you define success and fulfillment, and how have these definitions evolved over time?

8. **The Role of Mentorship and Role Models in Career Development:** Danielle's narrative touches on the influence of family entrepreneurship. Talk about the impact of mentorship or role models in your career development. How have these relationships guided your career choices and aspirations?

9. **The Value of Self-Investment and Continuous Learning in Entrepreneurship:** Danielle's success as an entrepreneur was partly due to her commitment to learning and growth. Share your thoughts or experiences on the importance of self-investment and continuous learning in professional development. How have education, mentorship, or other forms of learning contributed to your career?

10. **Creating a Positive Impact and Legacy Within the Community:** Danielle's work as an entrepreneur also focuses on contributing to her community and providing support to others. Reflect on how you aim to or have created a positive impact within your community through your career or personal initiatives. What motivates you to contribute, and what legacy do you hope to leave?

Dr. Latisha N Carter Blanks

"For I know the plans I have for you declares
the Lord, plans to prosper you and not to harm
you, plans to give you a hope and a future."
Jeremiah 29:11

The year was 1979 and the setting was a local shopping center. A three-year-old me was shopping with her parents and her older brother. Being that I was three, I guess I got tired of shopping and my dad and I took a rest on a bench outside of one of the stores. An older Caucasian gentleman sat on the bench next to us and struck up a conversation. During the course of the conversation, he asked me, "What do you want to be when you grow up?" I proudly replied, "A doctor."

His next question threw me for a bit of a loop; "What kind of doctor?" he asked.

I replied, "A Black doctor; what else?" I didn't know at the time that there were different types of doctors. All I knew was that I wanted to be a doctor and that I was Black. I have always been a bit of an Angela Davis, power-to-the-people type of woman, so maybe I was sneakily trying to tell him that Black folks could be doctors too. I'm not sure if my three-year-old brain was really reaching that far, but I would like to think that it was.

This was the first of many times that I verbalized out loud (perhaps declared!) that I wanted to be a doctor. Although I doubt I could have stated it this way back then, that day I began manifesting it until it came to fruition on June 6, 2002.

And so my journey to medicine began.

I grew up in the Brightmoor Neighborhood on the west side of Detroit. I was a product of a two-parent, middle/working-class home. I never really realized as a child that I didn't have "everything." My parents always made it feel like we had everything even when we may have been lacking. In fact, I never even really realized that I grew up in Brightmoor, because I was always told that I lived in the Eliza Howell Community, not really realizing that Eliza Howell was simply a section within Brightmoor. Brightmoor itself was a tough area, but in my mind, Eliza Howell was not. Looking back, I guess I lived my life in a self-made bubble.

It wasn't that I somehow believed I was better than the kids who lived in Brightmoor, but I held on to the fact that although I didn't live in the "fancy" neighborhoods like Rosedale Park, Palmer Park or Sherwood Forest, that I was somebody, too. I have always been of the mind that it doesn't matter where you come from, it only matters where you're going. Keep your eyes forever focused on the prize and keep marching forward.

High school can be one of the most challenging times in a girl's life. You are trying to discover yourself, and learning how to deal with new-found independence, while at the same time you're faced with the challenges that come with changing friend circles, social media and other things that can cause distractions in your life.

Like you, I am a product of Detroit Public Schools. I am a graduate of the Renaissance High School Class of 1994. Renaissance was a gift in my life. Renaissance allowed me to be my best self, while also cultivating my self-worth. One amazing advantage that I discovered during high school, well really after graduating, was that it was extremely gratifying to see so many teachers and staff who looked like me and they encouraged me to be authentically me. It was also amazing to see so many of my peers, young, gifted and Black, striving for excellence.

For my undergraduate degree, I attended Alabama State University (ASU). ASU is a Historically Black College or University (HBCU). ASU was Blackity, Black, Black, Black! It was a glorious thing to see the first time I stepped foot onto the ASU campus.

While at Renaissance, I applied to several universities. I wasn't really committed to going to one in particular. All I knew for certain was that I didn't want to go to The University of Michigan because my older brother was there and I wanted to get out of his shadow.

Never in my wildest dreams did I imagine that I would be attending ASU. Alabama State University is highly regarded as one of the highest-ranking public universities in the country. Being accepted was a dream come true. I frequently pinched myself that I was actually attending ASU.

The opportunity to attend ASU sort of fell into my lap. I was in church Sunday school and the instructor, who was an alumnus from Alabama State, asked if anyone in the class knew of any high school seniors who might be interested in applying to ASU, and even better, receiving scholarship money. I sheepishly raised my hand and stated, "I'm a senior and I would love to apply."

This was a defining moment that I now look back and say was what catapulted me to the next level. I applied and was awarded a full scholarship to ASU. My family had always believed in me and while I worked very hard in school to get good grades and my SAT scores were high, we were still surprised when we were notified about my full ride.

Attending ASU was a big adjustment for me. I had never really been away from home for any significant period, and I had difficulty making new friends and keeping an old friend I had known since elementary school. The pressure was considerable, and I almost gave up several times.

I cried many days during my freshman year. I just wanted to go home and be in the sanctuary of my comfort zone. My mother, and biggest supporter did not let me give up. She pushed me to stick through it. She continually encouraged me to not allow others to define me, and despite how I was feeling, she reminded this was only a short leg on my journey and to keep my eyes focused on the ultimate goal of attaining my M.D. degree.

Alabama State University proved to be the best place for me. In my sophomore year, I pledged Delta Sigma Theta, Sorority, Inc. This placed me within a like-minded group of women who had my back. Pledging and being around these women changed my life for the better. What I am saying is now that you have a mentor and a sounding board, find your tribe. It doesn't have to be a sorority, but it should be those individuals who have your best interest at heart and vice versa.

I learned many valuable lessons in my undergraduate years that kept me going and that I will impart to you. Find yourself a sounding board. It might not be your mother. It may be your father, a grandparent, a sibling, an aunt, an uncle, or a teacher. It's very important you find someone who can re-center you when your focus becomes blurry. I was willing to give up what could have ultimately been everything because I was lonely, scared and felt out of place, but my sounding board re-centered my mind and I was able to push through.

Three more things I want you to realize: one, speak up! Don't allow shyness or fear to determine your future. Had I never spoken up that day in Sunday school, I never would have been awarded the scholarship, and I can't say what my future would have turned out to be.

Two, follow the money! Undergraduate school is just one portion of your journey. Do not accumulate mountains of debt to obtain your undergraduate degree. Search for scholarships and grants. If getting into a good four-year school isn't an option straight out of high school, take classes at a local community college at half the cost and then transfer those credits later.

Three, find yourself another student at school you can bear your soul to: someone you trust and who trusts you to do the same. This person is someone you can cry with, pray with, and someone who will push you toward your destiny—especially when you think you've run out of steam and don't think you can make it.

The journey to becoming a medical doctor can be long and difficult. The ultimate prize is, of course, rewarding and worth it. Going through it is another story. I was told by many that coming from an HBCU, I wouldn't get into medical school. I never allowed this to discourage me, I trusted God even in that situation because God knew the desires of my heart and He wanted what was best for me all along.

For me, my Christian upbringing allowed me to fully trust God for His provision because He has you covered, even in the small stuff. I was always a good student, but I was never a good test taker. The entrance exam to medical school, also known as the MCAT, was a beast. My first score was terrible. Yet again, I had hit a bump on the road along my journey to becoming a doctor. However, enter my sounding board, who stood steadfast and reminded me that I had come too far to give up now.

While away at a summer externship at Johns Hopkins University in Baltimore, I decided, along with another student, to take a prep class and retake the MCAT. I needed to improve my score significantly to have a chance at getting into medical school. My score jumped five points after taking that class and I applied to eight medical schools the following fall.

I was only granted an interview at three of them:

1. Meherry Medical College in Nashville, TN
2. The University of Alabama (UAB), Birmingham, in Birmingham, AL
3. Wayne State University School of Medicine (WSU) in Detroit

I interviewed at Wayne State University last. I had already been placed on the waiting list at Meherry and had not yet heard back from UAB. I was discouraged, worrying whether I would reach my ultimate goal.

Was it true that coming from an HBCU, I had a disadvantage? I almost let self-doubt creep in again, but I stood on the Word of the Lord in Proverbs chapter three verses five and six, which reads: "Trust in the Lord with all thine heart and lean not unto thine own understanding in all thy ways acknowledge Him and He shall direct thy paths." I was admitted to Wayne State University School of Medicine and graduated on June 6, 2002. My journey to medicine was complete. I had many bumps along the way, along with countless numbers of things that could have stopped me. I almost lost hope—many times! I almost gave up; I had haters tell me that I couldn't do it, but that was the fuel I needed to keep striving.

Remember, it doesn't matter where you came from, it only matters where you are going. It doesn't matter what your mother did or what your father did; it only matters what you do! People talk about generational curses of teen pregnancy, falling into the wrong crowd, etc. Don't fall for this. Some people can only be what they see, but right now you see that you are the epitome of Black Greatness. Look in the mirror each day and say you are worth it. Don't let your haters distract you. Push forward toward the mark.

Before you know it, graduation has arrived and suddenly you find yourself having to make some tough decisions. What will you do next on your journey? For you to make the most of your high school years, remember to use the time you have wisely. I encourage you to make new friends and cultivate healthy relationships. Use every opportunity to learn something new. Find a mentor, someone who will stand in your corner and push you along the way. This is the beginning of your future, and you're literally laying the foundation for it right now. Four years may seem like an eternity, but those years go by fast and you will be soaring on to new heights before you know it. Take the lessons that you learn with you and build on them as you journey through life.

Dr. Latisha N Carter Blanks

Dr. Latisha N Carter Blanks is a Pediatric Medicine Specialist in Northville, Michigan. She graduated with honors from Wayne State University School of Medicine in 2002. Having more than 22 years of diverse experience, particularly in pediatric medicine, Dr. Carter-Blanks affiliates with no hospital, and cooperates with many other doctors and specialists in the medical group Regents Of The University Of Michigan.

QUESTIONS

1. **Early Aspirations and Self-Identity:** Reflect on an early memory when you expressed a dream or a goal, much like Dr. Carter-Blanks declaring she wanted to be a "Black doctor" at three years old. How does this memory influence your current aspirations, and how does your identity shape your dreams?

2. **Navigating Childhood Environments:** Dr. Carter-Blanks grew up in a neighborhood she perceived differently from its reality, thanks to her family's perspective. Think about your own childhood environment. How has your perception of where you grew up influenced your outlook on life and your aspirations?

3. **High School Experiences and Self-Worth:** Like Dr. Carter-Blanks' time at Renaissance High School, high school can be a formative period. Reflect on how your high school experience has contributed to your self-worth and your pursuit of goals. How have teachers and peers influenced you during this time?

4. **The Importance of HBCUs in Personal Growth:** Attending Alabama State University, an HBCU, was a significant part of Dr. Carter-Blanks' journey. Consider the role of your educational institution in shaping your personal growth. How has it influenced your understanding of identity, community, and ambition?

5. **Defining Moments and Opportunities:** Dr. Carter-Blanks' story includes a defining moment that set her on the path to Alabama State University. Share a defining moment in your life that significantly altered your path. How did it come about, and what impact has it had on your journey?

6. **Overcoming Challenges in College:** Transitioning to college was challenging for Dr. Carter-Blanks, involving homesickness and self-doubt. Recall a time when you faced significant challenges in an academic or personal setting. How did you overcome these challenges, and what support systems did you rely on?

7. **Valuable Lessons for Personal Development:** Dr. Carter-Blanks shares several key lessons from her journey, such as speaking up, following the money, and finding a trusted confidant. Reflect on the most valuable lesson you've learned so far in your journey. How did you learn it, and how has it shaped your approach to future challenges?

8. **The Journey to a Professional Dream:** The path to becoming a doctor was long and filled with doubts for Dr. Carter-Blank, but she persevered. Discuss your journey toward a professional or personal dream. What obstacles have you encountered, and how have you dealt with doubts or setbacks?

9. **Influence of Faith and Persistence:** Faith played a crucial role in Dr. Carter-Blanks' success. How has faith, spirituality, or a deeply held belief system helped you navigate tough times? Share an example of how this support has guided you through a difficult decision or period.

10. **Empowerment and Facing Adversity:** Dr. Carter-Blanks emphasizes empowerment and the importance of not letting one's background define their future. Reflect on a time when you faced adversity or doubt from others about your abilities. How did you use this as fuel to continue striving toward your goals, and what message do you have for others who may be in a similar situation?

Angelique Peterson-Mayberry

"Be anxious for nothing, but in everything by
prayer and supplication, with thanksgiving,
let your requests be made known to God."
Philippians 4:6

I've always been told that diamonds shine bright, but only after a gruesome process of extreme heat. Well, if I shine a little now, it's truly because God has kept me despite some of the heat I've encountered. I know everybody's definition of "heat" may be different. Still, I can confidently say I've been through a few fires, and I'd love to share just one of those with you, with the hope that you, too, shine brighter after heated situations you may find yourself in.

As a new mother of two children, ages three and five, I thought I had a storybook family life. A husband, a daughter, a son and a family pet. That sounds good, right? Well, what I thought was a storybook suddenly turned into what seemed like a scary movie. After seven years of marital bliss, I was now faced with divorce. Divorce? No, not me. I had vowed not to go down the route that so many of my friends had traveled or, like me, had been products of, but I found myself there.

After a yearlong process that took me through several stages of emotions from hurt to sadness to anger to feeling ashamed to feeling sorry for myself to questioning God, I felt them all. I looked in the mirror daily, forcing myself to smile and be strong for my young children. But inside, I felt broken, and not many knew what I was going through because I dared not look like what I felt. If I did, many would've known.

Instead of giving in to my feelings, I quickly tried to occupy my time with "busy work" to avoid being alone with my thoughts so I would not be forced to deal with my reality. I joined every church group I could, signed up for numerous community groups, and volunteered at every function simply to fill my time. Plus, I liked how I felt around others because I didn't have to face my own situation. Still, this "roller coaster" could only go on for so long, and it would soon catch up with me and force me to face things head-on.

One evening, as I sat on my bed in tears, my five-year-old son entered my room. I quickly wiped my tears and acted normal, but it was too late. Every other time, I had managed to hide my feelings and depression from my young children, but this time, I failed miserably. Having my son console me and tell me everything would be okay gave me the strength I needed to get myself together. It was as if a huge burden had been lifted. I committed at that very moment to put all my energy into bettering myself, taking care of my children, and listening more to God, and that's just what I did.

Months turned into a year, and I reduced my outside activities to focus more on what truly mattered at the moment: myself, strengthening my relationship with God and ensuring that my children were emotionally and mentally okay. We'd get it if we needed help in any of those areas. Despite being raised to believe that your business was just that and that you don't tell anybody about your business or see doctors for "stuff" like this, I decided to go against both ideas. I immediately started going to counseling and shared my story with a few close friends who supported me in every way imaginable. This helped me pick up the pieces of my life that I previously viewed as broken. Aside from my immediate family, I now had a circle of "Sistas" who went with me to social events and prayed for me. Boy, was I lucky. I soon realized that it was meant for me to share my story and journey to help someone else, but how, why and when?

While attending bible study one night (instructed by my church's First Lady), the class was given a week to select a book of the Bible to read, meditate on, and present to the class. I reluctantly selected the book of Job, not knowing much about it. Still, I later felt like the book actually selected me because it was exactly what I needed to provide insight and hope in my situation. The book of Job is about a man and his strong dedication to God, despite losing everything in his life, from his family and friends to his riches and health. Yet, he continued to trust God despite the suffering and difficult times and stayed dedicated to him, so he was blessed with restoration of all he had previously lost and gained so much more. I instantly knew that I was having a "Job-like" experience in my life. My marriage was over, I had walked away from a beautiful home I loved, my car lease was up, and I was no longer friends with certain people. There were many similarities between my life and Job's. My heart was filled with hope as I remained uncertain but trusted God all the while. Then, sharing my story happened.

A church "Sista" of mine, which I will vow to say is most certainly prophetic, reached out to me one day, totally out of the blue and wanted to come by my house. I was hesitant but felt better whenever I was in her presence, so I let her come by. My life took a major turn after that visit. She told me that God had not forgotten about me, that I would be blessed, and I should continue to trust him throughout my situation. I was speechless because she didn't know my situation, so this was nothing but God. Before she left that day, we laughed, cried and prayed, and I felt so full. But she had an "ask" of me. She wanted me to attend a church women's retreat and minister through a song that had recently hit the gospel charts by Mary Mary entitled "God in Me."

I couldn't believe that she asked me to do this. I had been in the choir for years but never saw myself as a "soloist," so I told her I'd get back with her. I contemplated the "ask" for days and felt I almost owed her, so I agreed. I had never heard the song, so I had to listen to it, learn it, and feel comfortable ministering it to the women who attended the retreat. Listening to the song's first verse, I felt the lyrics mirrored my life.

"You're so fly, you're so high

Everybody around you trying to figure out why

You're so cool, you win all the time

Everywhere you go man you get a lot of shine

Boy, like a magnet, better yet, I have it

Everything you wear, people say they gotta have it

From the sweat suit to the white tee to the Gucci

You can probably say people wanna get like me

But what they don't know is when you go home

And get behind closed doors, man you hit the floor

And what they can't see is you're on your knees

So the next time you get it, just tell em'

It's the God in me"

Since I promised to do the song, I enlisted a few of my choir members who rarely told me no. and had them sing back up for me. Before I knew it, we were "rocking," but something else happened. At the song's end, I uncontrollably shared my entire story. What was I doing? Nobody else was supposed to know my story. I didn't even know some of these women, and others I would not have shared anything so close and intimate to me, so why was I doing it? I was sharing everything: the good, the bad, and the really ugly!

When I finished sharing, tears were flowing, but I noticed something. These same tears, which were once tears of pain and hurt, were now tears of joy, and others shared these tears with me. As we sat around at the end of the night, our Assistant Pastor approached me and thanked me for being so vulnerable and sharing. She said two women had come to her after I shared my story, with similar stories, and they were inspired to share their stories with others as well. They thought they were alone in their situations that mirrored mine, but my sharing really helped them. I instantly felt "flat-out" good. Who knew that my taking that uncomfortable step in sharing my "business" would encourage others? As I sat in bed in the hotel that night, I couldn't help but smile and thank God!

I later found myself receiving abundant blessings like Job. A year later, I met the man of my dreams, who is now my husband of eight years. I purchased a car I had wanted for a long time, moved into a beautiful home in a neighborhood I had always wanted to live in, and secured a new job that paid double what I was making before. Who would've thought? No one could have told me that during that hot and dark time, I would be where I am now, and I'm thankful for where I am.

As I look back, I'm even more thankful for the "hot spots" I encountered on my journey because without those, there may not have been an appreciation for where I am now and that "shine" people sometimes see within me. It's funny because when people see you shine, they have no idea of the "heat" that you went through to get that shine that shines bright like a diamond. So, for those who are in "heated" spaces, don't worry. You'll shine real soon; just stay faithful and trust God!

Angelique Peterson-Mayberry
President of DPSCD School Board

Angelique is native Detroiter, born and raised in a place that she's still proud to call home! As a 3rd generation United Auto Worker, the value and importance of EVERYONE'S hard work was instilled in Angelique at a very early age by her mom Sylvia, and spending extensive amounts of time at meetings, marches and protest that addressed a threat to fairness and justice, was a normal way of life.

As the first African American and first African American female to be elected to the trustee position of UAW Local 245, Angelique officially entered the world of politics at the young age of 25. As a former Employee Resource Coordinator; Community Relations Director; Women's Committee Chairperson; and Diversity Facilitator Coordinator, she takes pride in her rigorous diverse journey, and values every lesson taught and mastered along the way.

Dividing time between her two current positions as an Employee Engagement Strategist for Manufacturing Employees at Ford Motor Company AND as the President of the Detroit Public Schools Community District School Board, Angelique's deep commitment to optimizing organizational success that fosters a thriving workplace culture, AND intentionally prioritizing academic excellence of student welfare, remain her guiding principle and providing answers to her "WHY"!

Angelique has actively engaged in various community initiatives leveraging her skills to foster positive change, and through extensive community involvement, she has collaborated with diverse groups to address pressing issues and amplify marginalized voices. Mrs. Peterson-Mayberry's allegiance to diversity, equity and inclusion is evident in her work where she strives to create inclusive and educational spaces that celebrate the richness of human experiences. Over the years, Angelique has contributed to impactful projects that promote equality and empower underrepresented communities and with her multifaceted experiences, there's no doubt that she will continue to champion principles for a more united – respected – and HEARD community.

Aware of the importance of balance, Angelique spends time mentoring the young girls of Intonjane Institute on life-skills, worshiping and serving in various ministries at Fellowship Chapel Church, and family gatherings that are sure to yield unforgettable memories. Despite a demanding and oftentimes hectic schedule, Angelique remains a devoted wife of Chris and endearing mother of Brooklyn, Jorden and "fur-baby" Stormy.

Angelique takes pride in being wherever she's needed and praying that others are left in a better place somehow when she's gone, enriched by her service - her words - her actions - or simply her work!

QUESTIONS

1. **Resilience in the Face of Personal Challenges:** Angelique's story illustrates her strength during a tumultuous period in her life. Reflect on a challenging time in your own life. How did you manage to stay resilient, and what or who helped you navigate through it?

2. **The Role of Faith in Overcoming Adversity:** Angelique leaned heavily on her faith and her church community during her struggles. Discuss how faith, spirituality, or a sense of community has played a role in your life during difficult times. How did it help you find hope or solace?

3. **The Importance of Self-Care and Mental Health:** Angelique took steps to focus on her mental health and self-care by reducing her outside activities and seeking counseling. Reflect on how you prioritize your mental health and self-care. What strategies or practices have you found beneficial?

4. **The Power of Sharing Personal Stories:** After sharing her personal story, Angelique found that it resonated with others and even inspired them. Think about a time when you shared a personal experience with others. How did it feel, and what impact did it have on you or those you shared it with?

5. **Finding Strength in Vulnerability:** Angelique's decision to be vulnerable and share her story at a church retreat led to unexpected blessings. Discuss a moment when being vulnerable led to a positive outcome in your life. How did it change your perspective on sharing personal struggles?

6. **The Impact of Support Systems in Personal Growth:** Angelique credits her circle of "Sistas" and her church community for supporting her through her journey. Reflect on the support systems in your life. How have they contributed to your personal growth or helped you during challenging times?

7. **The Significance of Role Models and Mentors:** Angelique was inspired by the biblical story of Job and received encouragement from a prophetic friend. Discuss the impact of role models, mentors, or inspirational figures in your life. How have their stories or advice influenced your path?

8. **The Journey of Rediscovery and Personal Transformation:** Angelique's journey led her to rediscover herself and transform her life. Reflect on a period of personal rediscovery or transformation in your own life. What triggered it, and what were the key milestones?

9. **The Role of Music and Art in Healing:** Angelique found a unique way to express her journey and heal through performing a song. Discuss how music, art, or other forms of creative expression have played a role in your healing process or personal expression.

10. **Reflections on Blessings and Gratitude:** Angelique concludes her story with reflections on the blessings she received and her gratitude. Reflect on your own life. Despite the challenges, what blessings can you identify, and what are you most grateful for?

Toshalyn Erve

"I can do all things through Christ who strengthens me." Philippians 4:13

From the earliest memories I can recall, my love for writing has always been a huge part of who I am. My journey began as a fifth grader at Hubert Elementary School in the heart of Detroit's Public Schools Community District (DPSCD), where I wrote a play called Playground. This piece wasn't just a frivolous child's play; it was a touching narrative set against the backdrop of innocence and the lurking shadows of drugs and gang violence that plague too many of our communities. The main character, a boy swayed by peer pressure, succumbs to drug use, meeting a tragic end right there on the playground where childhood innocence once dominated.

While I was in elementary school, I was involved in numerous writing and poetry contests, each victory and participation fueling my dream to one day become a News Anchor on WDIV Channel 4 News in Detroit. I idolized Carmen Harlan, a paragon of journalistic excellence in Detroit. I even had the honor of visiting the studio and taking a snapshot at the iconic newsroom desk. These experiences weren't just moments; they were the building blocks of my dreams.

As I stood on the cusp of high school, entering a national writing contest in USA Today Magazine became a defining moment. My essay, a heartfelt reflection on violence in American schools, didn't clinch the grand prize, but being quoted in a national magazine was a victory all its own. It was a testament to the power of words and the importance of giving voice to our thoughts and concerns.

Unfortunately, my transition to high school at Cass Technical High School, a beacon of academic and extracurricular excellence, marked a period of dwindling confidence. My parents' constant comparisons to my academically stellar cousins, coupled with the competitive atmosphere at Cass Tech, conspired to erode my self-esteem. The school's rich tapestry of talents, from the Performing Arts Department's Broadway-caliber productions to the prestigious Dance Workshop and Performing Arts Guild, both fascinated and intimidated me. My fears whispered doubts, stifling ambitions of dancing or acting in my future.

High school became a balancing act between striving for popularity and navigating academic expectations. Despite the potential my teachers saw in me, my focus veered toward the social whirlwind that is high school life–sidelining the academic excellence I was capable of. The looming question of college and the financial realities of higher education were shadows I barely understood until my senior year approached.

1997 was a year of reckoning as I grappled with college applications, haunted by mediocre ACT and SAT scores—a reflection of the self-doubt that had taken root in my psyche. Yet, amidst these challenges, I learned a powerful lesson about the strength of our thoughts and words, as only God can present them. The positive affirmation I shower upon my son today, celebrating his intellect and potential, mirrors the mindset shift I wish I had embraced when I was his age and looking at my future. His academic and extracurricular achievements are a testament to the power of belief and encouragement.

The college application process was a whirlwind of hope and anxiety, leading to acceptance letters from several universities. Choosing Central Michigan University (CMU) felt like a step toward a future I had yet to fully envision.

Transitioning to Central Michigan University marked a significant turning point in my life. The freedom and challenges of college life offered a fresh start, a chance to redefine myself and my ambitions. My initial stumble, a disappointing GPA in my first semester that put me on academic probation was a wake-up call that academic success required more than just talent; it demanded discipline, focus and belief in myself.

This realization propelled me to seek out communities and platforms where I could hone my craft and advocate for the causes I believed in. Joining The Organization for Black Unity and becoming a staff writer for the campus newspaper provided me with a sense of purpose and belonging, connecting me with like-minded individuals who shared my experiences and intentions.

My college years at CMU were a critical time of growth and development, challenging me to confront my fears, embrace my passions, and pursue excellence with renewed vigor. The academic struggles and social triumphs of those years were not just milestones; they were the stepping stones to understanding my true potential and the endless possibilities that lie ahead.

Despite being on academic probation my first year, I was able to bring my overall GPA up to a 3.0 and make the Dean's List by graduation. It was one of the proudest moments of my life to walk across that stage and receive my degree. Given all the struggles I had had in both high school and college, I knew in my heart I had earned that 3.0 GPA.

Armed with my degree, I returned to my hometown, naively expecting the job market to welcome me with open arms. How mistaken I was! After a fruitless job hunt that stretched over months, desperation led me to a temporary employment agency with some pretty interesting assignments. From assembling pizza kits for Little Caesar's Pizza to performing janitorial duties, I found myself questioning the worth of my education. The irony of my situation was not lost on me: here I was, a college graduate, wondering if all those years of study would be worth it.

Yet, I held onto the belief that God had a bigger plan for me, far beyond what I could see. This belief was put to the test when I applied for a factory position at The Bing Group, only to be met with a surprising response. The human resources manager, recognizing my potential, hesitated to put me into a role that she felt I was overqualified to perform. Despite my eagerness to accept any job, she urged patience, promising something more fitting.

True to her word, a more suitable opportunity presented itself at Detroit Chassis LLC (DCP), a company playing a vital role in Ford Motor Company's supply chain. The role of purchasing administrator was a glove fit, not just for my skills but for my spirit too. The interview with the Purchasing Manager felt less like an evaluation and more like a meeting of minds. Landing the job filled me with an indescribable joy.

DCP was not just a workplace; it was a community. Owned by two African American brothers, it was empowering to be surrounded by professionals who shared my heritage. My role as purchasing administrator was multifaceted: from managing the reception and processing purchase orders to creating and leading The DCP Observer, our company newsletter. This publication, born from my initiative, not only connected our employees but also reached the desks of our clients at Ford, becoming a symbol of our collective voice.

Despite my contributions and the accolades from the executive team, advancement eluded me. After five years of wearing multiple hats but remaining in the same position, the lack of recognition and progression began to wear on me. The daily grind, marred by negativity, took its toll on my spirit.

In the fall of 2007, I left DCP and got a job with White Construction, also Black-owned, that resonated deeply with my personal goal of uplifting my community. The prospect of contributing to another Black-owned enterprise filled me with a sense of purpose and pride. However, my tenure at White Construction mirrored my experience at DCP in more ways than one. Despite the smaller scale of the company, the elusive promise of career advancement remained just that—a promise unfulfilled. Yet, amidst the familiar roles, my passion for storytelling and community engagement flourished as I took the helm of the company newsletter, a role that brought me immense joy and satisfaction.

My time at White Construction was cut short just over a year later/ A casualty of the Great Recession of 2008, I was laid off. This period of my life was marred by personal and professional upheavals, including a painful breakup with a longtime boyfriend I had been living with, and returning to my parents' home. This return, though born out of necessity, blossomed into a period of profound personal growth and familial bonding. Amidst the economic downturn, I found solace and purpose in caring for my ailing grandmother, who apart from my parents, was the love of my life.

She passed away in February of 2009. I was very close to my grandmother, and I am thankful that God gave me the time to assist my mom with caring for her and to be able to cope with her death. I've learned never to question God. I have questioned him a few times in my life about things that have happened, but it always ended up being a blessing in the end.

The ensuing years were a testament to resilience and faith. Despite being laid off for over two years, I navigated the roller coaster ride of unemployment with grace, helped significantly by extended benefits and an unwavering belief in divine providence. As always, I knew God had my back.

My journey took a new turn in June of 2010 when I joined Chrysler, now known as Stellantis at the Jefferson North Assembly Plant. While the assembly line work is a far cry from my desires, it provides a stable foundation during uncertain times. The simplicity and routine of the job, however, brings about a growing restlessness—a yearning for a challenge that matches my capabilities and ambitions.

Throughout this journey, my mother's unwavering support and encouragement were my guiding light. Her persistent belief in my potential as a storyteller, despite my own doubts, planted the seeds of a dream I had yet to fully embrace. The notion of writing a book once dismissed as a fanciful idea, began to take root, fueled by the extraordinary circumstances of 2020. The global pandemic, a time of loss and isolation, also became a crucial time for reflection and transformation. Encouraged by my mother's faith in me, I started to envision a narrative that could encapsulate not just my journey, but those of others.

As the world grappled with unprecedented challenges, I found myself at a crossroads, contemplating the power of storytelling as a means to connect, heal and inspire. The question was no longer about whether I had a story worth telling, but how I could use my experiences to illuminate the paths of and for others. In the silence and solitude of a world paused, I discovered my voice and the courage to share it, guided by the belief that even the most ordinary lives are woven with threads of extraordinary resilience and grace.

However, it was when I asked other women to join me in sharing their stories that I realized the importance of believing in myself enough to move forward with my idea for an anthology.

The culmination of my journey is my tenure at Stellantis , where the factory floor allows me financial freedom and the ability to hope for my son's future. Encouraged by my mother's unwavering belief in my potential, I took the bold step of writing a book that encapsulated my experiences, insights, and the lessons learned along the way. But more than my own journey, Black Women Manifesting Greatness Through Education: The Detroit Anthology represents the journeys of some pretty amazing women—women I'm honored to know. This book is something much bigger and more important than myself.

This book was not just a personal achievement but a message of empowerment and hope to others, particularly Black women, underscoring the importance of education, resilience, and the pursuit of one's dreams.

Reflecting on my journey, from the playgrounds of Detroit to the publication of my book, I am reminded of the transformative power of dreams and the importance of pursuing them with courage and conviction. The challenges I faced, from the self-doubt of my high school years to academic and professional setbacks, were not impediments but catalysts for growth and self-discovery. My story is a testament to the belief that our beginnings do not define us; rather, it is our unwavering pursuit of our hopes and dreams, and the lessons we learn along the way that shape our destiny.

Today I see more than a path marked by trials and triumphs; I see a testament to God's unwavering presence in my life. My story, rich with challenges and victories, is living proof of His grace, guiding me through every storm and lighting my way with hope and love. This journey has been a co-creation with the Divine, each step imbued with faith, each chapter a shared narrative with the Creator.

Toshalyn Erve

Author of *Black Women Manifesting Greatness Through Education; The Detroit Anthology*

Toshalyn Erve's journey from the playgrounds of Detroit to the pages of her book, Black Women Manifesting Greatness Through Education: The Detroit Anthology, is a testament to resilience, passion, and the power of storytelling. Toshalyn brings over 18 years of diverse experience, with 14 of them in the automotive industry. Her forward-thinking, team-oriented approach reflects her deep commitment to contributing to and uplifting her community.

From her early days at Hubert Elementary School in Detroit, where she pennedher first play, to her academic and professional challenges and triumphs, Toshalyn's love for writing and storytelling has been the constant thread weaving through her life's tapestry.

Amidst the trials and triumphs of her career and personal life, Toshalyn's role as a mother has remained paramount. Her dedication to nurturing her son's intellect and potential reflects the lessons learned from her own life.

Black Women Manifesting Greatness Through Education: The Detroit Anthology is not just a book; it is a clarion call to Black women everywhere to recognize and embrace their power, resilience, and potential. Through this anthology, Toshalyn honors the journeys of remarkable women, including her own, to illuminate the importance of education, perseverance, and the pursuit of dreams. Her story, rich with challenges, achievements, and a deep-seated belief in God the creator and the divine, serves as a beacon of hope and inspiration.

QUESTIONS

1. **The Importance of Early Passions:** Toshalyn's journey into writing began in elementary school. Reflect on an early passion of yours. How has it influenced your path, and do you still pursue it today?

2. **Navigating Academic and Personal Challenges:** Toshalyn faced academic and personal challenges during her high school years. Share a time when you encountered similar obstacles. How did you overcome them, and what did you learn about yourself?

3. **The Power of Positive Affirmation:** Toshalyn emphasizes the positive affirmation she gives her son. Reflect on the impact of positive affirmation in your life. How has it shaped your beliefs about yourself and your abilities?

4. **Seeking Purpose and Direction in College:** Toshalyn's college experience was marked by a quest for purpose. Discuss a period in your life when you were searching for direction. How did you find your way, and who or what provided guidance?

5. **The Role of Community and Support Systems:** Toshalyn found a sense of community and support at Central Michigan University. Reflect on the communities or support systems that have been pivotal in your journey. How have they contributed to your growth?

6. **Overcoming Professional Setbacks:** Toshalyn experienced setbacks in her career but remained resilient. Share a professional setback you've faced. How did you deal with it, and what lessons did it teach you?

7. **Resilience and Self-Belief:** Navigating Life's Pivotal Moments: Toshalyn's journey is marked by moments of profound self-discovery and resilience, culminating in the publication of her book and her impactful role at Stellantis. Reflect on a pivotal moment in your life when you had to harness your inner strength and believe in your potential to overcome a challenge or seize an opportunity. How did this experience shape your path, and what lessons did you learn about perseverance and personal growth?

8. **The Impact of Mentorship and Encouragement:** Toshalyn's mother played a crucial role in encouraging her writing. Discuss the impact of mentorship or encouragement in your life. How has it helped you pursue your goals?

9. **Finding One's Voice Through Writing:** Toshalyn used her experiences to illuminate the paths of others through writing. Reflect on how you've used your talents or experiences to help others. What drove you to do so, and what impact did it have?

10. **The Significance of Sharing Stories to Inspire:** Toshalyn created an anthology to empower and inspire others, especially Black women. Reflect on a story, book, or narrative that has inspired you. How did it change your perspective or motivate you to take action?

CONCLUSION

Dear Reader,

Black Women Manifesting Greatness Through Education: The Detroit Anthology is a vibrant mosaic of resilience and achievement, showcasing the diverse journeys of women who, despite the challenges posed by the Detroit Public School System, have forged paths of remarkable success. This anthology is intended to serve as an empowering guide for incoming freshmen, offering hope and practical advice for navigating a school system that may not have the best reputation.

A common thread throughout these essays is that the women had to rise to the occasion if they were going to succeed in this challenging environment. Below I have summarized what I was able to get out of these essays. It's my hope that you can take these suggestions and apply them to your unique needs. You have more tools available to you than we did when we were in high school. I suggest leveraging them for even greater success.

Navigating the Educational Landscape

An incoming freshman in the Detroit Public Schools, or any lower-ranked school system, should enter with an awareness that their journey will be unique. It's crucial to understand that the reputation of a school doesn't dictate one's potential or future success. These stories illustrate that success is a personal journey, often carved out of determination, hard work, and a willingness to seize opportunities despite external circumstances.

Steps for Maximizing High School Years:

- Embrace Education: Recognize the power of education as a transformative tool. Despite any systemic shortcomings, focus on what can be learned and how it can be applied to future goals.

- Seek Mentorship: Connect with teachers, counselors, or community leaders who can provide guidance, support, and advice. A mentor can help navigate challenges, offer academic support, and open doors to opportunities.

- Utilize Resources: Leverage available resources, including tutoring, online courses, and technology, to supplement learning. Libraries, community centers, and online platforms can provide additional educational materials.

- Get Involved: Participate in extracurricular activities, clubs, or sports. These can develop skills, foster relationships, and provide a well-rounded educational experience.

- Set Personal Goals: Define personal academic and career goals early on. This clarity can guide decisions and maintain focus through high school years.

- Build Resilience: Learn to view challenges as opportunities for growth. Resilience is key in overcoming obstacles and achieving long-term goals.

Discovering a Future Path

Determining a career path in a challenging school environment involves introspection and exploration. Engage in activities that align with personal interests, volunteer in various fields, and seek internships or shadowing opportunities. These experiences can provide insights into potential career paths. Utilize career counseling services and attend college fairs to explore further educational opportunities and career options.

Resisting Negative Influences

Staying focused on education amid negative influences requires strong self-discipline and a supportive network. Surround yourself with peers who share similar ambitions and values. Engage in positive activities that reinforce academic and personal growth. Remember, the choices made in high school can significantly impact future opportunities.

Leveraging Technology and Education Resources

We're living through an era where technology plays a crucial role, so it's important to utilize online resources to enhance learning. Platforms like Khan Academy, Coursera and educational YouTube channels can provide supplemental knowledge and skills. Technology can bridge gaps in the educational experience, offering access to a world of information and learning opportunities beyond the classroom.

Seeking Guidance from Experienced Individuals

Mentorship can be a powerful tool for young women navigating challenging educational environments. Mentors, whether teachers, family members or professionals in desired career fields, can provide invaluable guidance, support and real-world insights. They can help identify strengths, recommend resources, and offer advice based on their experiences.

In conclusion, I hope my anthology underscores that success in the face of adversity is not only possible but achievable through perseverance, resourcefulness and a proactive approach to education. It's a testament to the fact that a school's reputation doesn't define one's destiny. With the right mindset, tools, and support, young women entering the Detroit Public School System, or any challenging educational environment, can carve out their paths to greatness and make their mark in the world.

With my deepest appreciation and warmest regards,

Toshalyn Erve

ACKNOWLEDGEMENTS

It's been quite a journey. This book has been four plus years in the making and I am so proud of myself for finally accomplishing my dream of becoming a published author. I'd like to thank my Heavenly Father first and foremost because without him this book or nothing else is possible.

I'd like to thank my mom who has always been my number one fan and supporter. She is the reason I wrote this because she kept pushing me to write a book and she never gave up on that dream for me because she knew my story needed to be shared with the world.

I'd like to thank my dad for just providing the laughs and positive energy needed at times to push through when things got tough.

To my son Braylon for giving me the motivation and the drive to want to do better and be the best mom that I could be to set a great example for him.

A special thanks to all of my contributors: Angelique Peterson-Mayberry, Aina Watkins, Ariane Bigby, Brittany Rhodes, Caron Recker, Danielle Smith, Kawana Baldwin, Kerrie Trahan, Joyce Sanders, Katrina Perryman, Colonel Robin Massenburg, Officer Malinda Cook,Sommer Oliver, Dr. Christie Hogue, Dr. LaTisha Carter-Blanks, Dr. Kali Keller, Dr. Shawna Patterson-Stephens, Dr. Sonya Franklin-Burney, Dr. Joslyn Harmon and Dr. Lashonda Fuller for seeing my vision with Black Women Manifesting Greatness Through Education: The Detroit Anthology and wanting to share their stories and be a part of it.

Thanks to my beta reviewers; Anthony Bostick, Chad "Sir Wick" Hughes, Natalagia Sims, Terrence Southern and Tinnica Favors.

Huge thanks go to my book designer Sanja Džadžević and Dr. Bridget Cole Williams for writing an inspiring foreword for my book.

To my sister-in-law Danielle who is the sister I never had. I want to thank you for always having a kind or supportive word during some rough times during this book writing process and just some turbulent times in my life, you have always been there.

Last, but definitely not least, I'd like to thank my book mentor and friend, Sarah Ratliff, for all that you have done to make my book project a success. You took me under your wing and never let me give up on my dream, even when things got too difficult and frustrating to give me direction when I didn't know where to go next. Thank you for sharing your impeccable knowledge and expertise on this entire book writing process and thank you for sharing your resources and all of your time. You are truly amazing.

Sincerely,

Toshalyn

Printed in the USA
CPSIA information can be obtained
at www.ICGtesting.com
LVHW021813050424
776549LV00003B/544